THE
SPEYSIDE
HOLIDAY GUIDE

Ernest Cross

First Edition 1993

For Pat, who puts up with me.

Other books by Ernest Cross:-
Walks In The Cairngorms, Luath Press Ltd.
Short Walks In The Cairngorms, Luath Press Ltd.

THE SPEYSIDE HOLIDAY GUIDE

By

Ernest Cross

LUATH PRESS LTD.
BARR, AYRSHRE KA26 9TN.

CONTENTS

ACKNOWLEDGEMENTS

In a world that seems to become increasingly brutish day by day it is always a comfort and a relief to escape to the gentle and more leisurely life-style of Speyside. People there still have time for talk, and they accept my, no doubt, irritating intrusions with unfailing patience and good humour - that alone is reason enough for going there.

Wherever I go I meet with unfailing courtesy and patience, and I gratefully acknowledge the help and assistance received from the individuals and organisations in Strathspey. They are many and varied, and include Tourist Board and Local Authority officials, shop keepers, hoteliers, Youth Hostel staff, guides in distilleries and other attractions, employees of the various nature conservancy organisations, visitors, and numerous local residents.

There is a special word of thanks for Mr. Jack Richmond, of Newtonmore, who has spent a lot of his valuable time trying to pass on some of his encyclopaedic knowledge of shinty to a mere Southron.

SPEYSIDE AREA MAP

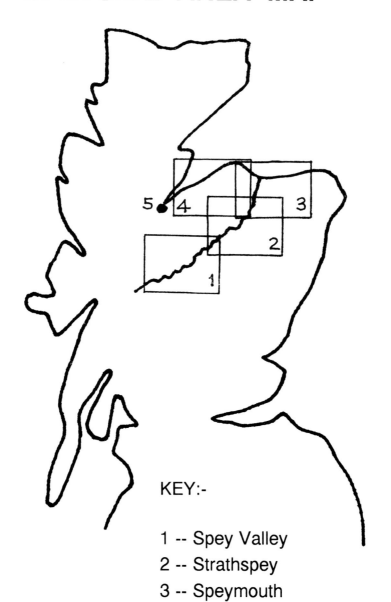

KEY:-

1 -- Spey Valley
2 -- Strathspey
3 -- Speymouth
4 -- Laich Of Moray
5 -- Inverness

SHELTER STONE CRAG -- from Cairngorm

INTRODUCTION

From the remote northern slopes of the Grampians, and out into the sea in the Moray Firth, a mighty river flows through an enchanting land. There are wild hills and majestic landscapes. There are lonely moorlands where the only sounds are of running water, a curlew's cry, an eagle's bark, and the wind's mournful sigh. There are ancient strongholds and stately mansions in peaceful river valleys, there are idyllic woodlands, and clean and quiet beaches, too. And all within a stone's throw of the delightful Georgian towns and villages that were built and developed here after the '45.

The Spey means different things to different people. To some it conjures up the memory and the expectation of great fishing. To others it is the home of the finest whiskies. Others, still, will associate it with the grandest, the most majestic, and the most romantic countryside in Britain. All will agree that there is nowhere else quite like it anywhere at all.

The Spey is very nearly the longest river in Scotland, and it is only a little shorter than the Tay. The Spey falls over ten feet in every mile, which is a very steep gradient for a river. It also has many mighty tributaries, which all increase the rate and volume of the river's flow. Consequently, the Spey is the fastest flowing river in Britain, as the ghillies who haul up the salmon boats against the stream will ruefully confirm. Indeed, the force of the water is so great, that the river accelerates all the way to the sea, and it is tidal for only about half a mile inland from Spey Bay.

There isn't really any particular place called 'Speyside', and to the locals the entire river valley is Strathspey. But the Tourist Board and other organisations have effectively created three sections of river valley called Spey Valley, Strathspey and Speymouth. To minimise confusion for visitors, these arbitrary divisions are used within this guide. It is assumed that Speyside includes them all, and a substantial area of adjacent countryside as well. This brings in the Laich of Moray, and a section of the coast that straddles Spey Bay. Inverness has been thrown in for good measure, since no visitor should depart without experiencing the charms of the sedate and gracious capital of the north. Together, they constitute a holiday area unique in Britain, and in this mini-Eden of the North a journey from the sunny beaches of the Moray shore to the sub-arctic wilderness of the Cairngorm plateau need take only a couple of hours or so. At the other extreme, it can take a lifetime. In between, there is a delightful amalgam of moorland, field and forest, and many interesting villages and towns.

Throughout the region the local residents are a cheerful and friendly folk who make the stranger welcome. They are ready to share the good things of their life; and life here is very good. This is an area that appeals to the walker, the golfer, the fisherman, the photographer, the naturalist and the artist; indeed, to the outdoor enthusiast of any and every sort. And, if enjoyment of the coast and countryside should pall, there is splendid shopping in the towns and an abundance of leisure activities and cultural pursuits. The high quality of Scottish cooking is well known, and good food and good company abound.

Each section of the guide has its own general introduction, with a map and useful information. This is followed by a gazetteer of towns and villages, plus the occasional chapter on a particular feature of the locality. There are details of interesting local activities that casual visitors often miss - Shinty for example. There is also some information about the rich and varied wildlife of the region - much of it unique in Britain, and sometimes in the world. There are separate sections devoted to particular activities and attractions. Some, in list form, provide details of items mentioned in the body of the guide. Together, they should provide plenty of ideas for days out in good weather and not so good. In short, there are many, if not all, of those things that can add a further dimension to a holiday. For those who wish to know more about Speyside, there is a reading list.

The guide has many references to the historic past, and no apologies are required for that, since history affects the people and the landscape in many, often very subtle, ways. Speyside has a varied, rich and colourful history, and the ramifications of events that happened here long ago are often still apparent. History explains, for example, the quite marked variation in dialect here and there across the region; the locations of the distilleries and the serene Strathspey towns; and why the various castles and stately homes are where they are. Thus an understanding of the past often helps to explain the present.

That, then, is the basis of this guide, which, in company with the river, starts in the mountains, and progresses through Strathspey to the sea. In the process it encompasses a roughly triangular area from Dalwhinnie in the south, and with Inverness and Cullen as the northerly extremes. Obviously it cannot be comprehensive, but it aims to detail and describe many things likely to interest the visitor, good places to visit, and things to do. It is intended to provide the answers to many of those questions that arise during a holiday, and which often entail a great deal of hunting for information and consequent wasted time.

At the start of Daniel Defoe's *Tour Through the Whole Island of Great Britain*, published in 1724, he said: '*If this work is not both pleasant & profitable to the reader ... the fault must be in the author's performance, and it cannot be in any deficiency in the subject*'. That applies with a vengeance here, and, as is usual in a guide book, the views, opinions, errors and omissions are the author's own. However, details of events and similar items were correct only at the time of writing, and no responsibility is accepted for later changes.

MAP NOTES

The sketch maps in this book should be regarded as 'scene setters' because, for various reasons, they cannot provide the amount of detail needed to locate many of the attractions of the region. They are intended to provide sufficient information to enable the required information to be found on a proper map.

The Ordnance Survey produce the most detailed maps available at whatever scale is used. For a broad-brush view of the region the OS 1 : 250,000 North of Scotland map is possibly the best, but there is serious competition at this level from the AA, Dunlop, Bartholomew and many other publishers.

More detail requires a larger scale. Bartholomew used to produce excellent maps at 1 : 120,000, and the entire Speyside area was covered by the following maps, which were probably all that the majority of visitors would need:

Sheets 51, 55 & 56

Second-hand or remaindered copies are worth searching for.

The most exacting motorists and cyclists will be satisfied by the OS 1 : 50,000 Landranger maps. They show every road and track, and serve as good general walking maps as well. The following five maps cover the area except for Inverness & Cullen:

Landranger 27, 28, 34, 35 & 36

Hardened walkers will demand the 1 : 25,000 Wayfarer maps, which are probably best obtained on the spot.

TRAVELLING

GETTING TO SPEYSIDE
By motorcar

The majority of visitors come by road, and the relatively large number of villages and towns means that Speyside has an excellent road network. In the north of Scotland all roads seem to lead south to Inverness. From there it is simply a matter of choice. The A96 runs east along the south side of the Moray Firth, and through the Laich of Moray. It goes on from there to Speymouth and on to Aberdeen. The A9 runs south, through Spey Valley, and other roads go north and east from there through Strathspey.

From Aberdeen and the east coast, the A96 leads straight to the north side of the region. The A939 Lecht Road, engineered by the 18th Cent. occupying troops, leads through Avonside to Grantown on Spey. From England, the A9, also created as a military road, scythes through the heart of the Grampians and into Spey Valley.

From Argyll and Lochaber, in the west, drivers have a choice of routes. The Glen Spean road by Loch Laggan meets Spey Valley at Laggan Bridge. The alternative is a long but scenic drive through Glen Albyn, and by the waters of Loch Ness to Inverness.

From England, the usual approach is by the A9. This great trunk road was recently rebuilt, and now provides effortless, if occasionally frustrating, travel. By driving up the western side of

England, using motorways, it is possible to travel from London to Inverness without passing through a town anywhere *en route* - they are all by-passed. The only problems with the A9 are the 60 m.p.h. speed limit, and the very limited number of dual carriage-way stretches. Many large lorries use this road, and overtaking opportunities are limited. This often leads to bunching and frustration for car drivers. Be patient, fall back, and enjoy the glorious scenery.

By bus

Regular express coach services operate between many towns and cities in the United Kingdom. Several buses serve Speyside. The main operators are Caledonian Express - 0738 33481, Scottish Citylink - 041 3329191, and Stagecoach - 0738 29339.

By train

From London King's Cross there is a through train service to Inverness that also serves Inter-City stations in eastern England. The west coast route, from London Euston, is being gradually run down, although British Rail say that this is not the case. There used to be many through trains to Inverness. Now they only run to Edinburgh, and Speyside-bound passengers have to go via Glasgow or Stirling and change to a Sprinter. In the skiing season it is now impractical to use the train because there is really no room for ski equipment on these local trains. Keith, Elgin, Forres and Nairn are served by the line from Aberdeen to Inverness.

Train service and ticket details from Scotrail - 041 2042844, or any manned BR station.

Hertz hire cars can be collected at any BR station. Scottish reservation details from Aberdeen - 0224 210748, Edinburgh - 031 5575272, and Glasgow - 041 2487733.

By air

Scheduled services from a number of British and other European airports fly into Inverness: Dalcross - 0463 232471, and Aberdeen: Dyce - 0224 722331. Hire cars can be organised to meet flights - Inverness: Avis - 0667 62787, Europcar - 0667 62374

Aberdeen: Budget - 0224 725067, Hertz - 0224 722373

GETTING AROUND SPEYSIDE

By motorcar

The most popular and most convenient form of transport is a car, and the entire region is served by a network of excellent roads. There is a bonus, too, in that traffic away from the two main routes of A9 and A96 is generally light, even at the peak of the holiday season. Because travelling is so easy there is a tendency to try to do too much, so remember that it is easy to return next year for the things that have been missed. Keep an eye on the fuel gauge, because garages are scarce away from the main villages and towns, and many are closed on Sunday. Fuel is relatively expensive because Speyside is far from the refineries and main distribution centres.

By bus

Bluebird Northern, Cairngorm Chairlift Co., Grampian Council Transport and Highland Bus & Coach all operate local bus services on Speyside, but buses tend to be infrequent, and there is often a reduced service during school holidays. The principal Highland service in Spey Valley is between Aviemore and Tormore, via Nethybridge and Grantown on Spey, and there is (roughly) a bus every hour between 8 am and 6 pm. During school term time there are very limited services between Newtonmore and Aviemore, and Aviemore and Grantown on Spey via Carrbridge. There is also an Aviemore - Cairngorm Chairlift service.

Bluebird Northern operate a frequent service on weekdays between Aberlour, Dufftown and Elgin. The Sunday service is poor. Grampian operate a weekday service between Aberlour and Knockando, and they coordinate the wonderful **Heatherhopper** and **Speyside Rambler** services. There are three Speyside routes: Spey Bay - Tomintoul, Elgin - Tomintoul - Aviemore, and Grantown - Tomintoul. Services vary with the day, and not all services run every day. With careful planning, it is possible to get about quite easily on these buses. They are most convenient for people walking the Speyside Way in sections - walk one way and ride the other. 'Tripper' tickets offer unlimited daily travel. Low's of Tomintoul run a variety of services & special tours. Bus timetable & fares information from local Tourist Information Offices or **Bluebird Northern** - 0343 544222, **Cairngorm Chairlift Co.** - 0479 861261, **Grampian Council Transport** - 0224 4580, **Highland Bus & Coach** - 0463 233371, **Low's** - 08074 333.

Main bus stations: Aviemore - 0479 810658, Elgin - 0343 544222, Inverness - 0463 233371, Nairn - 0667 53355.

By train

The railway runs through Spey Valley to Inverness, calling at Dalwhinnie, Kingussie, Aviemore and Carrbridge. The Inverness to Aberdeen line has stations at Nairn, Forres, Elgin and Keith. There are special holiday tickets available for travel in Scotland and within the region: **Freedom of Scotland, Heart of Scotland Rover, North Highlands Rover**. These tickets can be purchased at any railway station ticket office in Scotland.

Scotrail stations: Aviemore - 0479 810221, Dalwhinnie - 05282 219, Elgin - 0343 543407, Forres - 0309 72238, Inverness - 0463 233371, Keith - 05422 2517, Kingussie - 0599 4439.

Strathspey Steam Railway - 047983 692 - operates between Aviemore and Boat of Garten. There are many excursions.

By bicycle

Much of Speyside is ideal cycling country - steep gradients are uncommon and there are many quiet roads. Mountain bikes are very popular in rough country, and cycles can be hired in many towns and villages. Hire firms come and go quite frequently and are not listed, so ask at local Tourist Information Offices.

THE MAKING OF THE SPEYSIDE LANDSCAPE

As the last ice-age drew to its close Speyside would have been a truly awful place. Stripped down to bed-rock by the implacable grinding of the ice, the bare bones of the landscape were bathed by enormous lakes and washed by tremendous streams. These rivers, often several miles in width, coursed through a region of torn and shattered rock, with glacial debris lying everywhere. There were no people, no birds, no animals, no plants and no trees. There was no apparent life of any kind; just the rending and splintering sounds of tortured rock, the roaring of the wind, the thunder of water and the crack of breaking ice.

All this took place in a mere hiccup of geological time, and as the geological clock ticked once more the waters subsided and a muddy rubbish was left behind to form the basis of our soil. This was eventually populated by a variety of plants that grew from seeds and spores imported from gentler climes. They were carried on the wind and on the water, and were brought here by passing birds.

In geologists' terms the ice ages were recent happenings - the latest ended only some seven to ten thousand years ago - and the land is still reacting to the thawing of the ice. The glaciation was merely a modifying factor, which added fine detail to a basic skeleton that was created an unimaginably long time ago.

The predominant mountain-building activity, known as the Caledonian Orogeny, occurred some three hundred million years ago. In a period of cataclysmic change, which affected all the Highlands and also made the Alps, the existing rocks were uplifted and the Grampian mountains formed. This upheaval also left its mark in the uniform SW/NE alignment of such fault features as the Great Glen, the Findhorn and Spey river valleys, and the Highland Boundary Fault.

There are other deeply-etched features which do not conform to this alignment, and obvious local examples are Glen Garry, the Lairig Ghru, and the great trench of Glen Avon. In all these cases the natural grain and lie of the land have been emphasised and exaggerated by the sculpting action of moving ice, which has also produced such dramatic features as the great corries on the north face of Cairngorm.

The Roman general Agricola beat the Picts at the battle of Mons Graupus in 84 AD. The exact location of Mons Graupus is unknown. A Scottish historian, Hector Boece, of Dundee, used Tacitus's account of the battle for his *Historia Scotica*, published in 1527; but he misread the name as 'Grampus'. So that is how the Grampians were named - by a fortunate accident.

The Grampians lie between the Highland Boundary Fault and the Great Glen, a division which covers an enormous area, and which includes a complex mixture of mountain groups with rocks that differ greatly in appearance, constitution, character and age. They have virtually only two things in common: the time of their creation and their involvement in the last ice-age.

These mountains are the ground-down remnants of much higher hills and the great, Everest-like, peaks have gone, worn away by aeons of incessant weathering. Here, in the north-east, two great mountain masses remain. The Monadhliaths - great hills of grey Moinian granulite; and the Cairngorms - a pink granite massif that is a vast and undulating dissected table-land, where most of the highest ground was, apparently, untouched by the last coming of the ice.

The centre of the ice mass is thought to have been Rannoch Moor, and one mighty glacier, squeezed by sustained pressure from the Scandinavian ice fields to the east, moved north-eastwards along the line of the Spey. As the ice mass ground to a halt, and then started melting in retreat, it released the masses of sand, gravel and boulder clay that were bound up in the ice. These deposits were first laid down in lowland areas, like the Laich of Moray, and soils there have the greatest variety and greatest depth. In the mountains the thaw came later, and many of the soils were deposited as gravel layers in ice-dammed lakes.

The first vegetation would have been typically that of the tundra - still to be seen on the plateaux of the Cairngorm hills. This would have been followed by a mixed woodland of birch and pine, with willow scrub and alder carr in the wetter areas. Much of Spey Valley is still like this today, and it is a sobering thought that man has largely destroyed a glorious forest that once covered the whole of northern Britain. In the lower and more fertile lands of Strathspey and Moray the primitive forest would have been succeeded by oak and hazel woods, which were subsequently cleared by early man.

The post-glacial climatic change was extreme, and over a period of a few thousand years the sub-arctic climate gave way to a Mediterranean phase. It was much warmer than today, and the tree cover extended high up the mountain sides. This vegetation formed the soils that are now the moorland peats, and fluctuating climate is shown by the presence of large tree stumps preserved in the peat, high above the current tree-line. The peat itself, was, of course, also formed long ago from plant remains during another period of climatic change, from warm and dry, to a colder and wetter climate.

All of this is a gross simplification of what may actually have happened, but it should be sufficient to underline the fact that the present landscape is the result of a whole host of past events. The rivers have since cut down through the old glacial river beds, which are now the wide riverside fields and haughs that are such a distinctive feature of the region. The raised beaches north of Elgin, and the blown sands bound by pine woods, at Culbin, are further relics of Speyside's glacial past.

Geology dictates that mountain dwellers will be pastoral people, and that arable farmers must populate the more fertile lower-lying river valleys and the coastal plain where the climate is also less severe. It also explains why the buildings in different towns are made of different rocks, e.g. the pink granite of Grantown on Spey, and the Old Red Sandstone of Tomintoul. But, overall, it must be realised that the greatest modifier of the countryside on a superficial level has been and, indeed, still is, man.

It will be obvious that, from a geological point of view, Speyside is extremely complex, and this complexity provides a wide variety of landscapes. They include the sub-arctic tundra on the dissected plateau of the Cairngorms, the heathery grouse moors of Glenlivet and the Monadhliaths, the magnificent woodlands of Spey Valley and Strathspey, and the lush and fertile farmlands of Speymouth and the Laich of Moray.

The geology is something of a hotch potch which has not yet been sorted out, and professional geologists will be discussing and arguing about the region for years to come. At our level it is essentially a case of 'You name it and Speyside has got it', and it all adds up to a unique and attractive variety of hill and countryside, which is one of the important factors in our enjoyment of the region.

SPEYSIDE TOWNS & VILLAGES - A
feast of Georgian architecture

The Jacobite uprisings of 1715 and 1745 changed the face of the Highlands in ways which the principal antagonists could never have foreseen. Whatever personal opinions may be held on the subject - and they are many and varied and still controversial - there is little doubt, when viewed dispassionately, that the subsequent effects were largely beneficial to the ordinary people of the Highlands -- that is, to those who were left.

In the mountainous parts of the Highlands, towns were the exception and not the rule before the '45, and even now the Highland and Lowland concepts of towns differ, particularly in the matter of size. The traditional Highland way of life was geared to a largely outdoor existence, and it was usual to spend the summers with the cattle in the high pastures of the shielings. Being hunter/pastoralists, many people had a semi-nomadic lifestyle, moving with their beasts between the high and low ground, and then often herding them to the trysts before the cattle drives. Their 'houses' were often just shelter from bad weather, and the Isle of Lewis black house at the museum in Kingussie is typical of most Highland housing at that time.

The Clan system was a patriarchal society subservient to the chief, and a rigid hierarchy of clan members had a debt of service in the form of work and war. At the lowest levels the sub-tenants and cotters worked strips of run-rig land, which were used to grow oats and barley and a few vegetables. The ubiquitous black cattle were a major measure of wealth and prosperity, and were often the source of much trouble. The chief had the power of life and death, and severe punishment was often meted out for seemingly trivial offences.

A similar pattern would be seen with the, virtually peasant, farm workers and fisher folk on the lowland coastal plain. They, too, would have had a plot of land to till, in addition to their work for the Laird. The main difference would be houses gathered in a sort of village, unlike the isolated steadings in the hills.

So, however romantic the old clan system may seem in retrospect, it must sometimes have been quite awful at first hand. Heritable jurisdiction was not a particularly good system for maintaining law and order, but neither were the local magistrates courts in the England of that time. There was often much hardship and rough justice for ordinary folk - as James Macpherson's hanging goes to show. In the first half of the 18th Cent., in common with much of rural Britain, but made worse by a harsh and rigorous climate, this must have been a pretty miserable and squalid place in which to live.

There is no doubt that it was a difficult period, and the general poverty was exacerbated by the depression of the Napoleonic wars. It was not just the Highlands that were affected, but also the supposedly prosperous lowlands of the coastal plain. An early 19th c. visitor remarked that Elgin was idle and poverty stricken, and that poverty pervaded Forres like an evil spirit.

In the aftermath of the '45 the Government had sought to turn the Highlanders .....*from their idle and wicked practices to commerce and trade.* Essentially they wanted an end to internecine strife, to the harrying of the occupying troops, and to activities like cattle reiving. To this end sympathetic local landowners were encouraged to build new towns and villages and to foster the development of local industries.

There was a shortage of skilled craftsmen in the Highlands, and many of the artisans came from the Lowlands and from England, but the locals were used for general labouring. The building work, and labour in the subsequent small industrial and crofting townships must have done much to improve the local economy; but it certainly did not happen overnight.

It has been argued that it changed the Highlanders from pastoralists to peasants, but that's as may be. The policy seems to have worked in time, and the results are plain for all to see today. The following list of Speyside towns and villages, all either new or rebuilt in this period, is not at all exhaustive, but it reads like an architectural litany of the Georgian era:

(Charlestown of) Aberlour - 1812

Archiestown - 1760

Cullen - harbour, 1817

Dalwhinnie (inn) - 1730

Dufftown - 1817

Findochty - 1716 & 1833

Fochabers - moved, 1780

Forres - ancient burgh, rebuilt late 18th Cent.

Garmouth - ancient port, most prosperous in 18th Cent.

Grantown on Spey - 1765

Hopeman - 1805

Kingston - 1784

Kingussie - 1799

Nairn (new harbour) - 1820's

New Keith - 1750, and Fife Keith - 1817

Newtonmore - late 18th c.

Portgordon - 1797

Portknockie - 1677

Rothes - 1766

Tomintoul - 1776

It is interesting that Robert Adam, who achieved such world-wide renown as an architect and designer, was a son of William Adam - a famous architect from lowland Kirkcaldy - who rebuilt the fort at Inverness. William died in 1748, but the family firm retained their Government contracts, and the construction of the new Fort George at Ardersier, which started in 1748, was carried out by the Adam brothers. Robert, who was in his early 20's at this time, worked on the project before he went off to Europe in 1754, and there is no doubt that Fort George is where he did his first serious work. One of his last designs was also built on Speyside, and he created Balavil, near Kincraig, for 'Ossian' Macpherson about 1790, some two years before his death.

Speyside is a wonderful and fruitful ground for the architectural historian, or anybody else with an interest in attractive buildings. There is a preponderance of 18th Cent. new towns and villages, geometrical in layout and precisely planned; and the vernacular domestic architecture, with its simple lines, restrained decoration, and widespread use of dressed local stone, embodies the best features of the classical Georgian style. If the asphalt road surfaces and other trappings of modernity are ignored, it is like travelling back through a time warp for some 200 years.

All these towns and villages still have an austere and essentially Georgian air, but it tends to be leavened by the distinctive - almost Oriental - style of the distillery malthouses, and by a bit of Victorian opulence and comfort. There are also a few ancient and modern accents here and there. The modern, except at Aviemore, is usually contained and unobtrusive. The ancient is always picturesque, and is most evident in places like Cawdor, and in venerable ruins like

Elgin cathedral, and the various slighted and crumbled castles and strongholds.

The spacious and airy elegance of the hill towns and villages, almost always built in a pleasantly wooded countryside with undulating hills and pellucid streams, is complemented by the coastal towns and villages, which are set in rich farmland and are close to a glorious seaside. Blessed with a benign and relaxing climate, they combine happily to produce a distinctive and particularly attractive Speyside ambience. It has to be experienced to be believed.

REDSHANK

-17-

SPEY VALLEY - MAP & USEFUL INFORMATION

WEATHER REPORTS - 0898 500 424
TOURIST INFORMATION:
Aviemore - 0479 810363
Carrbridge - 0479 84630 Summer
Kingussie - 0540 661297 Summer
Ralia (A9) - 0540 3253 Summer
AA OFFICE:
Aviemore - 0479 810300
BANK OF SCOTLAND
Aviemore, Kingussie
Newtonmore
ROYAL BANK OF SCOTLAND
Aviemore, Carrbridge:
SCOTTISH TSB
Kingussie
CHEMISTS - Aviemore, Kingussie
EARLY CLOSING:
Aviemore - Wednesday
Boat of Garten - Thursday
Carrbridge - Thursday
Dalwhinnie - Wednesday

Nethybridge - Thursday
Newtonmore - Wednesday
Kingussie - Wednesday
DOCTORS:
Aviemore - 0479 810258
Kingussie - 0540 661233
DENTISTS:
Aviemore - 0479 810301
Kingussie - 0540 661280

PEREGRINE

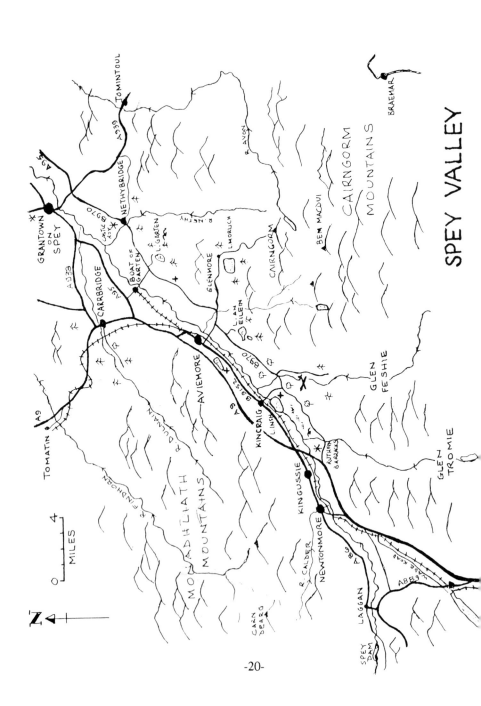

SPEY VALLEY

-20-

SPEY VALLEY - A Playground in the mountains

The Boar of Badenoch and the Atholl Sow stand at the summit of Drumochter Pass: twin sentinels that guard the entrance to an entrancing land. On the long climb to the summit, the road from the south traverses a dour and desolate landscape of glacial deposits, and the equally drab hills on either side merely add to the monotony of it all. There are countless acres of drumlin fields, and the gates that are used to close the road at times of heavy snowfall emphasise the desperate nature of the winter here.

As the road runs down towards Dalwhinnie and Newtonmore, the bleak moors and snow pole markers give way to the seemingly endless vista of Loch Ericht, away to the left, which heralds the junction with the old Wade road to Fort Augustus, via Laggan and the Corrieyairack Pass. Suddenly, the moors seem to lose their almost overwhelming dreariness, and in autumn a complex mix of yellow, green, grey, red, brown and purple provides a pleasant and polychrome harmony in a lower key.

The drumlin fields, which still lie all around, are a conglomeration of assorted humps and bumps, like a Lilliputian version of the Monadliaths. Ahead lies Spey Valley, an area with a long, colourful and varied history where man has left his mark throughout the ages, and the traces of this vivid past are evident to all who wish to see.

Prehistoric lake dwellers built their crannogs here, and there are the Iron Age hill forts of the Picts. There are memories of the old freebooting era; some sad reminders of the '45, and the remains of

Georgian military forts and military roads. There are relics of the early Celtic missionaries; and tiny churches and Georgian villages galore. There are also modern leisure and hotel complexes, and all the accommodation and amenities that present day holiday makers require.

This is a land of many contrasts, and the populous and fertile river valley is bounded by wild woodlands and rugged and untamed hills. The glacial origin of the valley is quite clear, and the roads, rail and river keep close company as their route is punctuated by the succession of delightfully quiet and attractive small towns and villages that lie between Dalwhinnie and Grantown on Spey.

To the west the Monadhliaths - the Grey Mountains - are a relatively trackless wilderness that is still unspoilt. To the east, beyond the Feshie, and dominating the finest remnants of the Great Wood of Caledon, the mighty Cairngorms rise in all their majesty. Technically a dissected plateau, this is the largest high landmass in Britain, and an almost legendary area of sub-arctic tundra. Surprisingly easy of access, it offers superb walking and climbing, and the best skiing in the realm.

From Newtonmore, the swift and sinuous ribbon of the Spey is the common thread that runs through the valley and unifies it all. Rising in the remote and stony fastness of the Monadhliaths, some 3000 feet up on the northern flanks of Creag Meagaidh, a little stream starts down towards the Corrieyairack Pass. The little stream is probably the real source of the river, although that honour is usually accorded to Loch Spey - further to the west and lower down, near to the watershed above Glen Roy.

Some miles to the east, the impressive bulk of Geal Charn dominates the north bank of Spey Dam. A rocky and lonely summit, it commands the bleak and windswept approaches to the Corrieyairack Pass. It also overlooks the lonely gathering grounds of two great rivers of the north. Beyond this mountain, in the remote and hidden fastness of the hills, innumerable burns run down to the north-east and then unite to become the scenic Findhorn. To the south, to the west and to the east, a myriad springs and streams form a crazy network of watercourses that eventually come together in the Spey.

The country is wide and open here, and the mountains, though very high, seem very far away. There is no pretty scenery on these moors, but there is undeniable grandeur all around. It is all to do with scale, and the vast and empty spaces about the headwaters of the Spey emphasise the enormous size and sense of wilderness that are so characteristic of the Highlands scene. This is a lonely landscape at the best of times, and it underlines the puniness of man. On a wet and windy, cold, grey winter's day one can only marvel at the hardiness and fortitude of General Wade's soldiers, who built the Corrieyairack road through such a harsh and barren wilderness in 1731.

The infant river has many tributaries, and by the old Kingshouse of Garvamore, Wade's magnificent twin arched bridge crosses a sizeable stream. Spey Dam, near to Laggan, collects these headwaters into a pleasant artificial loch, and the flow is then controlled by the dam. There is never any lack of water here, and the river flowing under Laggan Bridge, only a few miles from the source, is a dark and swiftly flowing stream.

From Laggan and on through Newtonmore the river is contained, but by Kingussie the country opens out and becomes almost gentle, and the ruins of Ruthven Barracks stand above a wide flood plain. The Truim and the Tromie boost the flow, and Loch Insh is actually just a widening of the stream. The Insh marshes are the largest area of fen and marshland in Scotland, and in winter, when the river is in spate, it is obvious why the region of Badenoch - the Drowned Lands - got its name.

The landscape here has changed again, and against the majestic backdrop of the Cairngorms and the Monadhliaths there is a sylvan wonderland of birch and pine woods, low hills, and willow scrub and alder carr. This is a staging point for many wading birds and waterfowl, and an impressive range of species can be seen as they pass through on their migrations every year.

The Feshie joins the stream beyond Kincraig, and from Aviemore the river runs dark and deep to the old ferry point of Boat of Garten, where it is now conveniently bridged. At the historic village of Nethybridge yet another confluence swells the stream, which flows on now through a pastoral and arboreal wonderland to the valley's culmination at the important and delightful town of Grantown-on-Spey.

CAPERCAILLIE

AVIEMORE - a new town & old birch woods

The Cairngorms have been attracting hardy climbers and hill walkers for a very long time, and skiers have been coming since the turn of the century. Most of the visitors in the past came by train, and Aviemore has always been a base for holidays, albeit on a rather small scale. Some 30 years ago Aviemore was a small village on the A9, a few miles along the road from Kingussie. It was the most important junction on the Highland Line, where the Forres branch left the main line to Inverness. Apart from the station there was a hotel, a garage, a cafe and some houses, and that was about it.

In the 50's Lord Fraser of Allander saw that the world was changing and, as a result of his initiative, a new and unique resort was developed here. Very much a child of its time, there can be no doubt about its birth date. The new Aviemore is brash and glitzy, and a slightly false and somewhat forced gaiety hardly hides a cheap and cheerful, and vaguely sleazy air. The white concrete slabs of the hotel tower blocks contrast starkly with the surrounding countryside, and there is an unmistakable and uneasy feeling that it is all in the wrong place. That said, there is no doubt that Aviemore grows on one and, whatever criticisms may be aired about the place, it attracts people, it satisfies a need, and it cannot be ignored.

So far, the Aviemore Centre seems not to have achieved its undoubted potential. Recent years have seen a succession of short-lived shops, restaurants and other enterprises, and there has been a general air of running down from what had never been a very high level in the first place. All that may now change. There is a rash of new developments around the town, and the Centre has a new owner. If the record elsewhere is any guide, Aviemore may at last turn into the popular and attractive resort envisaged by Lord Fraser so many years ago. It deserves to do so.

Aviemore is conveniently situated for many Spey Valley attractions, and good road and rail links ensure that Inverness and the whole of Strathspey are within reasonable range. The local holiday facilities are many and varied and, other than golf and water skiing, it would be difficult to name a sport or leisure activity that is not catered for in or near the town.

Craigellachie is the well-wooded low hill with the sheer and craggy rock-face that provides such an impressive natural setting for the Aviemore Centre. It is this rock, and not the fishing town in lower Strathspey, that figures in the Grant motto 'Stand fast Craigallechie'. That Craigellachie endures is beyond doubt, and it is central to the little National Nature Reserve, which covers about two square miles of delectable low hill country to the W. of Aviemore.

The reserve is notable on many counts, one of which is a resident pair of peregrine falcons that nest high up on the rock face near to the entrance to the reserve. There is a large area of birch scrub which is a habitat for many species of birds uncommon elsewhere in the area, for some reptiles and small mammals which are common but rarely seen, and for a variety of insect life that would be unusual anywhere, and which attracts naturalists from everywhere.

It is strange that an area so beautiful in itself is not over-run with other visitors. Not least of the delights of time spent here is that one rarely sees many other people. It is a little haven on the edge of the town, and most of the visitors encountered here seem to be specialist ornithologists, or other naturalists. This isolation is probably due to a combination of things, like the A9 which separates it from the town, ignorance of the access tunnel's whereabouts, and a lack of publicity.

Two paths lead to the tunnel, which was provided as the only access point when the A9 by-passed the town some years ago. One path runs from the main street, from a point between the Youth Hostel and a caravan site. The other path starts from a bend in a road on the Aviemore Centre, near to the Badenoch Hotel. It goes across the grass by a little lochan, and picks up the other path near to the tunnel.

Various short walks are possible in the reserve, and regular visitors soon create their own favourites. Probably the wisest course on a first visit is to follow a clockwise course around the nature trail on the finely graded path. This is constructed of gravel, stone slabs and duck boarding, depending on the terrain. It is beautifully done and maintained, and the 'viewpoints' are well chosen. There is nothing here of the artificiality so often evident on other nature trails. No numbered posts and set pieces, and apart from the path it is all as nature made it. A cheap and excellent explanatory leaflet can be had from the Tourist Information Office, but lack of the leaflet is no obstacle to enjoyment and understanding.

The birch is a widespread and hardy tree, and several species grow naturally in Britain. Silver birch is an import that has spread widely and hybridised with the native downy birch, and it is a graceful and beautiful species that enhances any area in which it grows. The woodland here is a rare and precious gem, which makes a very refreshing change from the seemingly ubiquitous conifers elsewhere.

Autumn is a splendid season here, and the reserve is exceptionally beautiful then as the yellowing leaves, when sunlit, provide a green, grey and gilded tapestry which is a vivid and unforgettable backdrop to the town. The quiet and contemplative stroller here will be rewarded with the sight and sounds of many unusual birds, moths, small animals and plants. It is all the more attractive for the marked contrast with the great pine forests nearby. Wander and wonder, and haste ye back.

BOAT OF GARTEN - Ospreys
and a steam railway

Between Kincardine Church and Boat of Garten vestiges of the old Caledonian forest appear beside the Spey, which wends its way majestically in a succession of deeps and boulder studded rapids. A very deep deep occurs by Boat of Garten which, as the name suggests, was once a ferry station. In 1898 the ferry was superseded by a bridge, which was itself replaced some twenty years ago by the present steel and concrete structure.

'The Boat' doesn't amount to much but it has a great deal of charm. A couple of hotels, some shops, a caravan site, and a few houses line the long and very minor road linking the A95 Aviemore to Grantown road to the B970. It is a quiet and peaceful place dedicated to tourism, and there is no shortage of things to do. The main activities concentrate on 'the great outdoors', and are concerned with fishing, golf, bird-watching and walking; and there are plenty of opportunities for them all.

A little place like this cannot be expected to provide a wide range of amenities, but it has plenty to offer for its size. There is a superb golf club that glories in its soubriquet 'Gleneagles of the North', but it has nothing remotely like the fuss and expense of that famous course.

Abernethy Angling Association offers salmon and trout fishing to resident visitors on several miles of the Spey and other local waters. It is also possible to hire canoes and, for something completely different, there is an off-road driving centre. The village is also ideally placed for the local skiing, both downhill and langlauf, and it is free from the frenetic bustle of nearby Aviemore.

Boat of Garten is also the headquarters and northern terminus of the Strathspey Steam Railway, and a programme of excursions and special events runs throughout the season. In addition to the scheduled services between The Boat and Aviemore, there are 'osprey' tours which provide the ultimate in nostalgia for transport buffs. The railway train is often pulled by steam, and a round trip to Loch Garten and the ospreys is provided in a vintage omnibus.

You can enjoy an excellent lunch on the train each Sunday and Wednesday, and that is a great delight, especially for those nostalgic about the days, not so long ago, when railways were **real** railways. Beer drinking railway enthusiasts will find their particular Nirvana at the end-of-May Beer Festival. There are excursions, a bar-marquee, and twelve assorted real ales for devotees.

The village was built when the railway came in the late 19th Cent., and the hotels and oldest houses date from then. The Highland Railway branched at Aviemore, and the line to Forres passed through the village. A further branch at Nethy Bridge connected with the GNSR Strathspey line.

The lines always needed tourists to provide an income, but the motor car speeded their demise. The end came in the 1960's when Dr. Beeching closed so many railway lines. That should have finished off the railway, but a group of dedicated enthusuiasts managed to acquire the rail bed to Grantown, and a steam service to the Boat started up in 1978. It has succeeded beyond all expectations, and it is now planned to extend the line to Grantown. There are souvenir shops at both stations, and there is an interesting little exhibition at Boat of Garten.

Ornithologists will need no introduction to the area, for at Loch Garten, just down the road, there is one of the great success stories of conservation. From a solitary pair of birds that nested here in 1959, the osprey population in Scotland has risen well into three figures. Ospreys need a lot of space, and there have been reports of birds prospecting for nesting sites as far south as the Lake District in England. There are other nests in Strathspey, but the only one that is accessible is here.

The RSPB has a 3000 acre reserve, and this is the place where it is very easy to watch the ospreys. In the comfort of the hide, a CCTV screen linked to a camera above the nest shows every intimate detail of the nesting habits of these beautiful birds. Thousands of visitors come here every year to be enchanted and captivated, and it is no exaggeration to say that Loch Garten is a place where bird watchers are hatched.

There is also a network of footpaths in the extensive woodland, and there are three delightful waymarked trails. One starts from the car park at the junction of the Boat and B970 roads, and the others are from the car parks by the osprey hide.

About three miles down the road to Coylumbridge, Kincardine church has an interesting history. The walls are very old, as a leper squint in the east wall seems to indicate, and there is also a strange hollowed boulder by the door that is possibly a font dating back to the Columban missionary days.

Legend has it that a 15th Cent. Laird of Grant was murdered by the Comyns when on a visit to the Wolf of Badenoch's son. The Comyns, pursued by avenging Grants and Stewarts, took refuge in the church. A burning arrow fired the roof, which was made of thatch, and the Comyns swiftly met their end.

The church remained a ruin for 400 years, but was restored in 1897. It is a peaceful place today, and a little shrub in the graveyard is a reminder of another romantic tale. In the 16th Cent. the 5th Baron of Kincardine married a daughter of Cameron of Locheil. On her death-bed she expressed a wish to be buried in Lochaber's soil, so some soil was sent to put into her grave. It must have contained some seeds, for the little shrub of dwarf elder, which normally grows in Lochaber but not in Strathspey, sprang up here soon after. It has grown by the churchyard ever since, and is known locally as the 'Baron's Lady's Flower'.

CARRBRIDGE - Landmarks, telemarks and old bridges

A quiet Highland village on the fringes of nowhere in particular, Carrbridge is a famous place in skiing circles. The first Scottish ski school was established here by the Austrian Klaus Fuchs, and the simple little monolith opposite the Struan House Hotel commemorates his life and achievements. The sport still flourishes in the winter months, and there is now a Nordic (cross country) ski school here as well.

This peaceful little village is also noted for the picturesque old bridge, to which it owes its existence. On an ancient corpse road to Duthill churchyard, it was built by the Earl of Seafield in 1717 to ease the passage of funeral parties across the Dulnain river. The original bridge, which was never used by pack horses, was badly damaged by floods shortly after it was built and had to be repaired.

It is often supposed that the bridge was built by General Wade, but this is not the case, and Wade was still an MP in England when this arch was made. The steps on the green by the bridge lead to a viewing point, and the prospect is pictured in many publications. It is an exquisite view that cries out for a camera.

There is a Wade bridge at Sluggan, which is about three miles away up the little road that goes past the station. The bridge is on the old military road to Inverness, and it can be the objective for a pleasant half-day walk.

Carrbridge nestles in glorious woodlands, and birch and pine add a heady fragrance to the summer air. There are many pleasant

OLD DULNAIN BRIDGE - CARRBRIDGE.

walks in the woods, but the best place to experience the forest is the Landmark Centre, by the A9 on the southern outskirts of the village. This attraction is deservedly popular with adults and children; it has a host of things to see and do.

There are various forest trails, not all of them on the ground; an adventure playground - not just for children; a sculpture park; and, most spectacular of all, a seventy foot high tower with a viewing platform way above the tree tops that gives stupendous views. The exhibition area tells the story of the local timber industry from its beginnings right up to the present day. A steam-powered saw mill helps to bring it all to life.

The little 9 hole course on the A983 can provide some entertaining golf; and fishing, pony trekking, and mountain bike hire are all available in the village. The village is also a noted winter sports centre. Langlauf enthusiasts have plenty of choice around the village, and the Cairngorms are only a short drive away.

Just off the Grantown road and near to Dulnain Bridge, the heather nurseries at Skye of Curr are worth more than a cursory visit. There are literally hundreds of different species and cultivars of Calluna, Erica, Daboecia and many other kinds of ericaceous plants. This is not just a place for keen gardeners, for there is also an excellent gift shop, and flowers, house plants and a tea room.

At Dulnain Bridge, on the road to Grantown, there is a notable example of the glacial features known as 'roches moutonees'. These smoothly rounded humps of rock - fancifully named from their supposed distant resemblance to sleeping sheep - nicely demonstrate glacial erosion. The moving ice - here travelling northwards - swept away all soft and loose material in its path, but left unaffected the material on the lee side of the rocks. This gave rise to the characteristic crag and slope effect so common in glaciated regions. Carn Eilrig, in the Cairngorms, is a good example of a glaciated hill, and these smoothed rock masses demonstrate the effect on a smaller scale. There is a car park and an explanatory display.

FAIRWINDS HOTEL

Carrbridge,
Inverness-shire
PH23 3AA
Tel: (047 984) 240
Roger and Liz Reed

Experience a true Highland Welcome. Dine on Scotland's Finest Produce:- Speyside Trout, Salmon, Venison, Cheeses and many others. Relax in pleasant comfortable surroundings in front of a real fire. Perhaps glimpse a shy Roe Deer from your bedroom. All our rooms are *en suite* and centrally heated. Our guests are assured of personal attention at all times. Vegetarian meals and packed lunches are available by arrangement. Sorry, no dogs.

Many activities locally, or just have a rest. Allow us to make
your holiday memorable.
Please write or phone for further details.

● ● ●
HIGHLY COMMENDED

AA
SELECTED

♔
RAC
HIGHLY ACCLAIMED

The Wade bridge at Sluggan is on the old military road to Inverness, and it can be the objective for a pleasant half-day walk. Park in the large car park near the Information Centre caravan in the centre of Carrbridge. Go right on the main street, cross over the bridge, then walk up the little by-road to the left, sign-posted for the station. The road is metalled, but once past the station there is a pleasant grassy verge to walk on, and the scenery is a constant delight with heather moorland, woods and fields alternating on either hand.

Two miles from Carrbridge, in the woods, a definite branch to the right leads through a gate to Sluggan bridge. Further on, at the edge of the wood, a track goes north to join the military road, and at a junction with another track the road plunges steeply down towards the river. This is Wade's old road, and it passes through a fine old birch wood. As the road approaches the ruined farmstead of Sluggan the woods give way to rough pasture, and the bridge is straight ahead.

'Sluggan' is the Gaelic name for a throat or gullet, and it will be seen that it is very apt just here. The valley closes in upstream, and there are steep banks on both sides of the river. Sluggan Bridge crosses the stream in a great soaring single arch above the white shingle, and there are little gates at each end to exclude suicidal sheep. The approach is bounded by odd clumps of trees: larch, birch and bird cherry, with an occasional rowan. It is all incredibly colourful in the autumn.

Over the bridge the old road goes on to Slochd and Inverness. The path back to Carrbridge is to the right, through more woodland. Cross the bridge and go right immediately beyond the tumbled ruins of an old building. A faint but definite track passes first through birch woods, and then through pasture and rough farmland to another minor road. This joins A983 near the golf course. Go right, and back into the village.

GENERAL WADE & THE MILITARY ROADS

Field Marshall George Wade was, by any standards, a remarkable man. Born in Ireland in 1673, he entered the army and was an Ensign in the 10th Foot Earl of Bath's Regiment in 1690. He had risen to the rank of Captain by 1695. In 1702, as one of the Duke of Marlborough's officers, he distinguished himself at the siege of Liege when his grenadiers stormed and captured the citadel. His promotion was rapid, and by 1708 he was a Brigadier, and was second in command of an expedition to Menorca.

Menorca has a rough and mountainous terrain, and when Wade arrived there were no roads. The expedition had great trouble with artillery transport, and Wade would have been quick to see that decent military roads were essential, and he may have served his road building apprenticeship here. In 1711 Wade was promoted to Major General, and he left to take command of the army in Ireland. It is almost certain that he gave a flying start to Richard Kane, Governor of Menorca from 1713 and famous, amongst other things, for his roads. When Wade retired from the army he became an M.P., first for Hindon, and then for Bath.

After the rebellion of 1715, the general disarmament of the Clans placed the many law-abiding Highlanders at the mercy of those few people who chose to live outside the law. The Jacobite cause rumbled on, and there was widespread discontent and many complaints and appeals to the King, especially from Lord Lovat. In 1724 Wade was recalled to the colours and sent to Scotland to sort out the problems.

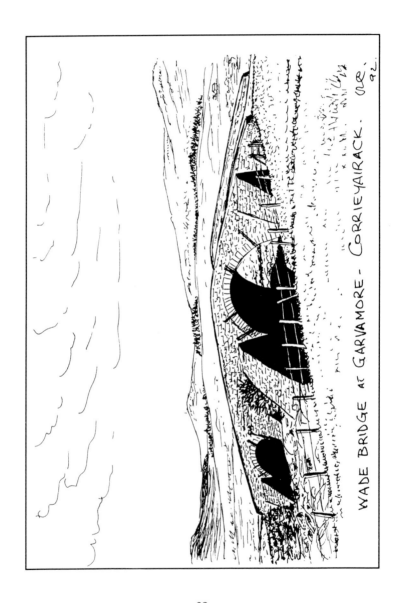

WADE BRIDGE at GARVAMORE - CORRIEYAIRACK.

On 3rd July 1724 Wade was personally commissioned by George I:

> 'Narrowly to inspect the situation of the Highlanders, their manners, customs, the state of the country in regards to the depredations committed in that part of H. M. dominions, to make special enquiry into the allegations that the effect of the last Disarming Act had been to leave the loyal party in the Highlands naked and defenceless at the mercy of the disloyal; to report if Lord Lovat's proposals were founded on fact; and to suggest such remedies as may conduce to the quiet of H.M. faithful subjects, and the good settlement of that part of the Kingdom'.

Wade wasted no time, and on 10th December following he reported that:

> 'Of the 22,000 men in the Highlands capable of bearing arms; 10,000 are well affected to the Government, the remainder have been engaged in rebellion against Your Majesty ..... the Highlands of Scotland are still more impracticable, from the want of Roads & Bridges, and from excessive Rains that almost continuously fall in those parts, which by their Nature and constant use become habitual to the Natives, but very difficulty supported by the Regular Troops. They are unacquainted with the passages by which the mountains are traversed, exposed to frequent ambuscades and shot at from the tops of the hills...' and so on.

On 25th April 1725 Wade was appointed C-in-C of Scotland. Thus began a third and legendary career during which this formidable man formed the Black Watch, and constructed a network of military roads and rebuilt the forts down the Great Glen. Wade's plan was to create a triangle of roads connecting the main forts in the Highlands, with access from the south along a road that is largely followed by the modern A9. The main route north was from Dunkeld to Fort George (Inverness). A secondary road was later made from Crieff via Aberfeldy. This joined the main road at Dalnacardoch, at the south end of Drumochter Pass, by the junction with the old Edendon/Gaick track to Ruthven.

Another road traversed the Great Glen along the east side of Loch Ness (now mainly A82, B852/862), and connected Fort William, Fort Augustus and Fort George. The final link, between Fort Augustus and the main N-S route, was built in 1732 on the line of the old drove road over the Corrieyairack Pass. Near to this junction, at Ruthven, Wade had renovated the old barracks in 1727, and added a stable block in 1734. This was part of his continuing policy of maintaining a strategic presence, whilst also providing decent and comfortable depots for his troops.

There was a touch of irony in the use of the military roads by Prince Charles Edward Stewart during the rebellion of 1745. Wade, by now a Field-Marshall, was an inactive by-stander in charge of an army at York as Charles campaigned into England, before finally retreating to defeat at Culloden at the hands of the butcher Cumberland. Making further use of Wade's roads, Prince Charles fled to France in 1746. Wade finally retired in 1748. In the years 1725 - 38 he had constructed over 240 miles of road and 30 bridges for not much more than £20,000. Equivalent to almost £500,000 a mile at today's prices, the roads were quite a bargain.

After Culloden the road building carried on, mainly under the supervision of Major William Caulfield. When they finished, the military had created over 1000 miles of new road. In view of this total, it may be wondered why Wade merits so much attention when he built the smallest mileage. The answer lies, of course, in his being the visionary and the innovator. The extent of his achievement may be gauged from the fact that, before him, only the Romans had built roads on such a scale, and, like Hadrian, he was the governor of a province. Simultaneously he was also the army commander, an engineer, and M.P. for Bath. Lesser mortals can always follow when a great leader has blazed the trail.

The forts had no real effect, and they were either ignored or destroyed by the Highlanders. But the roads and bridges built by Wade and his successors opened up the Highlands, and formed the basis for the roads we use today. Many of our modern roads, such as the A9, and the Lecht road to Grantown on Spey, largely follow the lines of the roads created by Wade and his successor, General Clayton. There are other stretches, long since redundant and overgrown, that can be followed as footpaths or hill tracks. Speyside has many examples of these, and interested walkers will find some fascinating and rewarding routes on the old Wade roads.

OSPREY

DALWHINNIE & LAGGAN - Cross roads of history

For northbound travellers on the A9 across Drumochter the grim brown moors seem never-ending, and the white walls of the distillery at Dalwhinnie are just about the first sign of approaching civilisation. The branch down to the village leads on to Wade's old road. Before 1729 the journey could only have been worse, and as soon as the military road was built from Perth to Inverness an inn was opened here. In those days it probably did good trade with the cattle drovers, whose herds of black cattle would pass by on their way south. Some two years later, in 1731, Wade completed his road from Fort Augustus over the Corrieyairack, and the two roads joined near the inn.

Queen Victoria was a notable early visitor, and she stayed here (incognito) for one night in October 1861, when on the third 'Great Expedition', this time to Glen Feshie. Afterwards she wrote in her journal: *'the worst was there was hardly anything to eat, only tea which I cannot take at night & 2 miserable starved Highland chickens! It certainly was not a nice, or very appetising supper. No pudding and no fun.'* So Queen Victoria was not amused. Her servants must have been even more disgruntled, for she also noted that John Brown and her two maids had to make do with the remains of the miserable chickens.

During the evening someone had discovered the identity of the guests, and at their departure in the morning they were seen off by a group of local people. The crowd was headed by the clan chief, Cluny Macpherson, and the royal party was piped away towards

Kingussie. The Queen's journal does not comment on the music, which is a pity, because the piper was Malcolm Macpherson - Calum Piobair - the greatest-ever player of the pibroch. Things obviously took a turn for the better after this visit, and in the 1870's the railway arrived and the inn, which is now the Loch Ericht Hotel, became a noted resort for fishermen.

The name *Dalwhinnie* is derived from the Gaelic word for a meeting place, and in the past the wild country hereabouts was a traditional gathering-ground of the clans. The name could also be associated with the inn, the roads, or the cattle drives. The village has a beautiful situation at the head of Glen Truim, and there are wonderful views of Ben Alder, often snow bedecked, at the far end of lonely Loch Ericht.

The residents of the village might reasonably challenge Tomintoul's claim to be the highest village in the Highlands, since they are both at about 1200 feet. The people of Tomintoul would no doubt say that Dalwhinnie is too small to be a village. It is indeed a tiny place: just a few houses and shops, a couple of hotels, a garage and the station, so there is room for doubt.

What is not in doubt is that Dalwhinnie - on the River Truim - has the most elevated distillery in the country. Founded in 1898, it is now famous for a delicate malt that will be a revelation to those who think that the finest whiskies come only from the Spey. It is easy to judge, for visitors are welcome at the distillery between 9-30am and 4pm on Monday to Friday. There is an interesting guided tour and a free dram.

The A889 from Dalwhinnie uses Wade's old route to Laggan, which is a tiny hamlet at an important road junction - this time with the Corrieyairack and Fort William roads. It has a delightful setting at the foot of the Monadhliaths, and on the banks of the Spey near to its junction with Strath Mashie.

High above the confluence of the streams is the prominent and picturesque Iron Age hill fort of Dun da Lamh. It was occupied by

Pictish people, who recognised the strategic importance of this place, and the sheer size of their fortification provides some food for thought. Built on the edge of a steep crag, some 600 feet above the valley floor, the only reasonable approach is along the ridge from the south. The roughly triangular enclosure measures some 100 by 150 yards, and the walls are in places over 20 feet thick. They are also up to 9 feet high. And those are the remains that exist to-day! Clothed now in pines, and standing in splendid isolation on the flood plain of the Spey, it is an incredibly romantic and photogenic sight.

Although a quiet and peaceful spot to-day, there have been many exciting times here in the past. The first military use of the Corrieyairack road was not by Government troops, but by the Jacobites in 1745. When Bonnie Prince Charlie landed in the west and gathered his army about him in July, General Cope set out to intercept him. Intending to march to Fort Augustus, he heard that the Jacobites were in possession of the Corrieyairack Pass. This was a virtually impregnable position, so Cope and his army turned away and headed north to the fort at Inverness. It was a controversial decision at the time and, although cleared by a subsequent enquiry, he was under a cloud thereafter. 'Cope's Turn', by the junction of the Spey and Mashie, is marked by a clump of trees near the bridge to Dalchully House.

A year later, in somewhat desperate straits, the fugitive Prince Charles traversed the road once more. At the end of August he met up with the great Cluny - Ewan MacPherson - and spent some two weeks sheltering in the vicinity of Loch Ericht. Most of the time was spent in the hide-out of 'Cluny's Cage' on the south-east slopes of Ben Alder. In mid-September he slipped away, and by the 20th he was back on the west coast, from whence he sailed away to France.

These are places for a quiet holiday, with fishing and excellent walking all about. Even the most indolent can get the feel of the Corrieyairack, because the road has now been surfaced beyond Garvamore and right up to Melgarve. The summit of the pass is about four miles from here on what is still recognisable as a road, and the streams can be forded where the bridges have gone. This is rough country, so do not go if the weather is bad.

RED DEER

KINCRAIG, INSH & THE FESHIE - a sylvan wonderland

Superficially, Kincraig doesn't amount to much at all: just a few houses, a hotel and a shop that straggle along a lane linking two minor roads, midway between Aviemore and Kingussie. It is a peaceful little place amongst the birch and pine woods at the foot of Loch Insh, but, although tiny, it has a wealth of interest out of all proportion to its size.

On a little wooded knoll by the loch, Insh Church stands on a site of great antiquity. The present building dates from the 1790's, although the foundations and the fabric of the walls are much older than that. It is the churchyard that provides a clue, for it is roughly circular. This is a characteristic seen also at the similar churches of Alvie and Kincardine, and often indicates a church built on a pre-Christian site. The theory is that the early missionaries sometimes built their chapels within the existing stone circles of their erstwhile Pagan converts.

There are three rare treasures in this remarkable little church, two ancient and one quite modern. The massive granite block against the south wall within the entrance porch looks like a rude and simple font. It was, indeed, used for baptisms, and it is, most probably, a Pictish relic. Is it imagination, or are there traces of some sort of inscription or carving on the flat front face of the stone? A hollowed granite block, very like this one, lies outside the doorway of Kincardine church.

The little alcove in the east wall, inside the church, holds a silver platter and a siver covered vessel of the early 19th Cent.

Above them hangs an oddly shaped and somewhat battered bell. Cast in bronze, and with an iron clapper, it is known as St. Adamnan's Bell. It is one of only five bells of its period in Scotland, and its shape and age are identical to those of the smaller iron hand-bells used by the Culdee monks.

The Culdees were missionaries, and they lived in Scotland during the 8th Cent. Their name is said to be derived from the old Irish *cele de,* meaning 'servants of God', which the 16th Cent. historian Hector Boece rendered as 'Culdee'. Thought to be about 1100 years old, this bell would have been made a long time after Adamnan's death, but there is no doubt that it is a missionary bell,

and may have adorned an early chapel here. A virtually identical bell in Edinburgh is attributed to St. Fillian.

The little church is, of course, dedicated to St. Adamnan, and it is quite possible that it was founded by him. One name for the knoll on which it stands is Ion Enonan, which means Eunan's Isle, and Enonan, or Eunan, is a familiar form of Adamnan. Adamnan followed Columba as a Bishop of Iona, and he was also the earlier saint's biographer. As Seton Gordon has pointed out, dedications to St. Columba and St. Adamnan usually go together, and the ancient foundation at nearby Kingussie is St. Columba's.

The windows of Insh Church are of clear glass, but the north window is far from plain, and it is adorned with a most beautiful engraving. The work of Helen Turner, it was dedicated in 1964, and depicts the glorious Cross of St. John, at Iona.

Like nearby Kincraig, St. Adamnan's church does not, at first sight, appear to amount to much, which proves, yet again, just how deceptive appearances can be. This simple little haven, set in beautiful woodland by a delectable loch, provides much to think about and ponder on.

The church at Alvie is, perhaps, even older than Kincraig, and is said to have been founded by St. Drostan, a nephew of St. Columba. There are other reminders that people have lived in the valley here for many thousands of years, and to the north of the A9, at Dalfour, midway between Alvie and Kincraig, there are remains of a massive ring cairn, some ninety feet in diameter. According to Mrs Russell, of Insh, a Pictish stone was recently discovered at nearby Dunachton, doing duty as a lintel in a barn. The name of Dunachton refers to the long-since-vanished castle of Nechton, thought to have been a Pictish chief. The stone now stands in the private grounds of Dunachton Lodge.

Speyside is noted for its wildlife, and it is doubtful if any other region of Britain of comparable size can match it. Naturalists of every pursuasion, both professional and amateur, come here to study

the plants, animals and insects, the variety and diversity of which are enormous. In the past the variety was even greater, and included animals like the brown bear and wolf. The infamous 'Wolf of Badenoch' got his name because wolves were a fact of everyday life in the 14th Cent. The last wolf in Britain was killed by the Findhorn less than 250 years ago.

The Highland Wildlife Park at Kincraig, off the B9152 on the way to Kingussie, is neither a safari park nor a zoo, yet it has elements of both. It has a collection of the wild animals and birds that are resident in Scotland now, and which lived here in the past but no longer do so. The parkland of about 250 acres is a reserve where most of the animals live in natural surroundings. It must be said that creatures like the eagles and wild cats do not seem to appreciate their luck in having a comfortable billet here, and they often look pretty fed-up with their lot. On the other hand, the otters are only too well aware that they are a star attraction, and seem to show-off endlessly when there are visitors around.

Although designed with mainly car-borne visitors in mind, pedestrians are catered for too, and a Land-Rover picks up from the entrance gate. The Visitor Centre has a variety of walk-round compounds housing smaller animals and birds, and the ponds support an interesting collection of resident and transient water-fowl. There are some surprises, and the lynx, bison and arctic foxes, all unexpected, represent animals that died out here several thousands of years ago.

Loch Insh is just a widening of the Spey, but its depth and fish population suggest that it is a kettle hole, formed by an ice plug at the end of the glacial epoch. This attractive sheet of water is popular with water sports enthusiasts, and canoes, wind-surf boards and sailing dinghies can be hired. The loch also provides good fishing. One unusual resident is the arctic char, a left-over from the icy past. A cousin of the salmon and trout, it is a deep water fish, and spends most of the year near the bottom at depths around sixty feet. The usual method of char fishing is trolling with a spinner and a heavy weight. Grilled char is a great delicacy, far finer in flavour than any other members of the salmon family. Loch and river fishing is also available on the nearby Alvie estate, as are shooting and stalking in the appropriate seasons.

The marshland, upstream from the loch, is actually a huge area of fen. Unlike the usual bog, this waterlogged peatland is rich in minerals, and the soil is not particularly acid. Between Ruthven and Loch Insh, an area some five square miles in extent tends to flood in the winter, and it provides an important wildlife habitat. The low mounds of glacial till support willow, alder, and hazel scrub, with patches of birch and rowan. The multitude of ponds, even in the driest season, attracts roe deer, herons, harriers, and many other birds. By Invertromie, on the B970, the RSPB Insh Marshes Reserve has a Visitor Centre, and the hides overlook a delightful stretch of river valley.

Bordering the B970 on the south side of the river, the undulating wooded hills of Inshriach Forest are a sylvan Paradise. Bordering the road, the great expanses of downy birch, a species that has been growing here since the ice ages ended, provide dappled shade on the hottest of summer days. In the autumn, for a period that is all too brief, they shine like pyramids of beaten gold against the grey, brown and purple backdrop of the hills.

Upstream from Tromie Bridge, a track leads for twelve lonely miles to Loch-an-t-Seilich and Gaick Lodge, which must have been one of the most isolated houses in Strathspey. The lodge replaced an older building that was the scene of a great tragedy when it was swept away by a mighty avalanche in January, 1800. From Tromie Bridge there are some pleasant short walks in Inshriach Forest and the Woods of Glentromie, and the whole area is a nature lovers' delight.

A minor road from Feshiebridge runs past the gliding strip, and continues south for six miles to Achlean. As the road emerges from the pine woods, not far from the farm, there is a dramatic change in the landscape, for Glen Feshie, that most beautiful of river valleys, is bounded by mighty hills. This little visited gem, which runs down the western margins of the Cairngorms, is one of Scotland's loveliest glens.

There is a slow transition from the bleak and hostile tundra of Britain's highest mountain plateau to the soft and verdant pastures by the riverside. Typical of the Grampians, the landscape bears the unmistakable stamp of its glacial past, but there is a marked contrast between this most delightful of river valleys, which provides a lonely but lovely walking route from Kingussie to Braemar, and those other N-S routes, the Lairig an Laoigh and the Lairig Ghru.

A broad strath of the softest green is dotted, here and there, with the brown and ochre mounds of ancient drumlins. Nicely rounded hills, with rocky scars and outcrops, provide a dramatic back-drop for the trees. Gnarled and knotted old Scots pines alternate with weeping birch and prickly gorse and junipers, and the river is always close at hand. In places there may be up to a dozen separate streams, and little lawns of lush green grass provide ideal picnic spots between the rills of icy water draining down from An Moine Mhor - the great moss.

English visitors who know The Lakes will feel very much at home because there is a very 'Lakeland' feel about it all, but the resemblance ends with that. There is a marked lack of tourist hordes, and a very different scale: Glen Feshie is simply vast. It provides plenty of space and plenty of scope for artists, walkers, naturalists, botanists, birdwatchers, and sundry other discerning folk. Seekers after solitude, they all can find here something very special in the peace and quiet, and in the absence of the frenzied activity that is now so apparent in other parts of the Cairngorms.

The wilderness is more apparent than real, and there was much activity here in the past. There are the remains of several farms, and there was once a thriving timber industry. Most of the old pines of Caledon were felled during World War I, but there are still many areas of pleasant mature woodland, with a mixture of both coniferous and broad-leaved trees. The glen is famous for its deer, and it is not uncommon to see herds of several hundred moving on the hill.

For the majority of those who know it, the mention of Sir Edwin Landseer's name will instantly evoke 'The Stag At Bay', which represents, perhaps, the pinnacle of Victorian genre painting. The original is now in Dublin, but the inspiration is all around in Glen Feshie. Landseer had the ability to combine pathos with a touch of cruelty in his pictures, and he was very successful. He was one of Queen Victoria's favourites, and he visited Balmoral and other Royal estates on and off over a long period. The Queen, who was herself an accomplished water colour painter, probably had lessons from him when at Balmoral.

Landseer rather enjoyed the sporting life and, although a rotten shot, he neglected no opportunity for deer stalking, and similar pursuits. He certainly had a great fondness for the Highlands, where he could both indulge his tastes and soak up the atmosphere for his pictures. Glen Feshie was one of his favourite places, and he had a bothy, or summer cottage, here.

From Achlean, a river-side track passes through some most attractive woodland to the bothy at Ruigh Aiteachain, some three miles to the south. Near by, and a little upstream, there stands an isolated chimney stack. Solidly built in local stone, it has its back to the hill, and looks over a shallow depression to the river. A trickle of ice cold and delicious water runs from a little spring near by, and it is easy to imagine the idyllic life here in the summer time. The chimney stack is all that is left of Landseer's bothy, which is likely to have been similar to its slightly smaller and rougher neighbour. Queen Victoria passed this way in 1860, and considered it a lovely spot. She was quite enchanted by the trees and the beauty of the view.

Landseer never married, but he was far from averse to feminine company, and is supposed to have had a romantic attachment to the Duchess of Bedford, who owned the cottage he rented in the glen. It is recorded that she was a frequent visitor during the sporting season. Sir Edwin and his aristocratic companion once were weather-bound here and found some time to experiment in the kitchen. The result was, apparently, 'Duchesse' potatoes - true or not, it makes a charming story.

A track goes steeply uphill to the east of Achlean. It leads to the summit of Carn Ban Mor - the big white cairn - and onto the great moss. A short way up this track, just beyond the fence, another track goes to the right through the pine woods, and to a most delightful waterfall at Badan Mossach. The name means a dirty, or messy, little spot, and never could a place more belie its name. This is the epitome of sylvan beauty, and it beguiles all who visit it. The old Scots pines here seem to be particularly attractive to crested tits, which are rare and most delightful little birds.

KINGUSSIE - Capital of Badenoch

The capital of Badenoch, and now a popular holiday resort, there was a settlement here in the 15th Cent., for this was originally the 'Kirk Town' of the then much more important village of Ruthven - more of which anon. The interesting little graveyard off Mill Road is probably the site of the original missionary chapel of St. Columba, which, it is thought, was in use 1400 years ago.

The present town dates mainly from the end of the 18th Cent. - and is another product of that great era of rebuilding in the Highlands. A brainchild of the Duke of Gordon, it was conceived as yet another textile manufacturing town. The industry was not a success, and it was only the coming of the Highland Railway, in 1870, that rescued Kingussie from almost certain oblivion and started its development as a holiday resort.

The name of the town, pronounced 'Kinyewsy', is a corruption of the Gaelic phrase 'The Head Of The Pine Wood'. The reason for the name is obvious, and the town has an enviable situation in an elevated setting at a point where the valley of the Spey starts to open out to the north. Built steep-to, on the flanks of Creag Beag, right at the foot of the Monadhliaths, the town is sheltered from the worst of the weather from the west. It enjoys a bonny prospect across the river to the Inshriach forest, and to the hills that enfold Glen Tromie and Glen Feshie.

This quiet and attractive town is another super holiday resort with good hotels, good eating, and good shops with friendly and attentive shopkeepers. It is one of the great attractions of the Highlands that people will always make time for a chat, and local

THE SILVERFJORD HOTEL
Ruthven Road, Kingussie, Inverness-shire.

The village of Kingussie nestles at the foot of Creag Bheag, in the splendour of the Spey valley. It is an ideal centre for touring and hill walking, and for all the other delights of the Highlands.

Here at the Silverfjord, quite simply we serve the best food around. Bar meals and dinners can be complemented from an excellent wine list.

When you stay with us, you will find that the rooms are very comfortable, (some with private baths), with wash basins, electric blankets, tea/coffee making facililties, and central heating.

For a friendly atmosphere with a personal touch.
Tel: (0540 661) 292. Guests 342.

businesses still maintain those old fashioned standards of service that are often just a dim and distant memory elsewhere.

There is much to do and see in the locality, but pride of place must go to the Highland Folk Museum, in Duke Street, near to the centre of the town. The museum has had a somewhat chequered history, and its creation and continued existence are due largely to the grit and determination of Dr Isobel Grant, who founded the enterprise on Iona in 1934. It came to Speyside during the war, and various universities and charitable trusts have lent a hand. It is now a flourishing, unique and evocative reminder of the life-style of a vanished world.

A Hebridean blackhouse provides an example of the sort of dwelling the Speyside locals had before the 18th Cent. re-building began. It isn't the usual dead museum piece, and visitors can cough their hearts out in the reek of the peats as delicious bannocks cook on the griddle. Also outside are a clack mill and a Victorian salmon smokehouse, but there aren't any samples from this. The farming museum has everything from primitive wooden hand tools to

Fordson tractors, and a blacksmith can often be seen at work.

A fascinating collection of artifacts and memorabilia of days
gone by provides a feast of nostalgia in the delightful ambience of
old Pitmain Lodge. There are tools and kitchen implements; there are
articles of clothing and pieces of furniture; old ornaments and old
documents; stuffed birds and animals, and many other reminders of
the past. The whole makes an absorbing and informative display.
There is usually someone doing something, like spinning or weaving,
and, again, this gives an invaluable insight of the days when one
could not just pop out to M&S.

Pony trekking is a regular summer activity, and tennis players
and bowlers can enjoy a game in the town. In marked contrast to
Newtonmore, the golf course here is in the mountains up the Gynack
Road. Designed by the legendary Harry Vardon, the 18 hole course
provides memorable golf in breathtaking surroundings. Badenoch

Angling Association offers a variety of excellent fishing on 12 miles of water. Coarse fishermen should note that Loch Gynack, nestling between the big and little Creags by the golf course, is reputed to contain huge pike - further details at Spey Tackle, or the newsagents in King Street.

Further afield there are water sports on Loch Insh, climbing and walking of incomparable quality in the Cairngorms and Monadhliaths, and skiing in the winter months. At the Dell, down by the river, winter sports enthusiasts tired of the pistes can watch a game of shinty. Or they may prefer the relaxation and quiet enjoyment of *aprés ski* in one of the many pleasant hotels in the town, as an alternative to the somewhat frantic pleasures in other resorts.

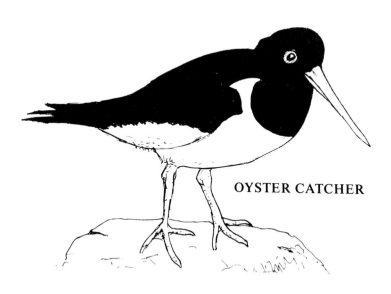

OYSTER CATCHER

RUTHVEN BARRACKS - The end of the Jacobite dream

Just across the river, on the B970 road to Insh, Feshiebridge and Nethy Bridge, the ruins of Ruthven Barracks stand in stark and solitary splendour on a substantial Norman motte. Nothing is known of its very early history, but by the 14th Cent. the Comyns had a stronghold here, and it was a major seat of the notorious 'Wolf of Badenoch', who burnt most of Elgin in 1390. The castle passed into Gordon hands, and it suffered destruction and reconstruction during a period of continual strife until its final demolition during the Civil War in 1689.

The present barracks were built in 1719 to house one of the garrisons stationed throughout the Highlands after the 1715 rebellion. Wade added the stables in 1734, and the presence of the troops may well have improved the incomes of the poor souls living in the clachan of Ruthven near the foot of the mound.

When Cope withdrew from the Corrieyairack and marched to Inverness, the Jacobites followed in force and laid siege to the barracks. No account of the action could improve upon that written by Sergeant Molloy, commander of the garrison of fourteen private soldiers. His account is preserved in a despatch written to General Cope, which reads as follows:

RUTHVEN BARRACKS - KINGUSSIE

Ruthven Redoubt, August 30th, 1745.

Honourable General,

This goes to acquaint you, that yesterday there appeared in the little town of Ruthven above 300 men of the enemy, and sent proposals to me to surrender this redoubt, upon condition that I should have liberty to carry off bag and baggage. My answer was, that I was too old a soldier to surrender a garrison of such strength without bloody noses. They threatened hanging me and my men for refusal. I told them I would take my chance. This morning they attacked me about 12 o'clock, by my information with about 150 men. They attacked Fore-gate and Sally-port, and attempted to set the Sally-port on fire with some old barrels and other combustibles, which took blaze immediately: but the attempter lost his life by it. They drew off about half an hour after three. About two hours after they sent to me, that two of their chiefs wanted to talk with me. I admitted, and spoke to them from the parapet. They offered conditions: I refused. They desired liberty to carry off their dead men: I granted. There are two men since dead of their wounds in the town, and three more they took with them, wounded as I am informed. They went off westward about 8 o'clock this morning. They did the like march yesterday in the afternoon, but came back at night-fall. They took all the provisions the poor inhabitants had in the town; and Mrs. McPherson the Barrack-wife, and a merchant of the town, who advised me to write to your Honour; and told me there were above 3000 men lodged in the cornfields west of the town last night, and their grand camp is at Dalwhinny. They have Cluny McPher-son with them prisoner, as I have it by the same information. I lost one man shot through the head, by foolishly holding his head too high over the parapet, contrary to orders. I prevented the Sally-port taking fire by pouring water over the parapet. I expect another visit this night, I am informed, with their pateraroes, but I shall give them the warmest reception my weak party can afford. I shall hold out as long as possible. I conclude, Honourable General, with great respect,

Your most obedient and humble servant,

MOLLOY, Sergeant.

As a reward for this spirited action the intrepid sergeant received immediate promotion. Six months later, the gallant Lieutenant Molloy faced an even more serious attack from a Jacobite army that fielded large cannon. He had little option other than to surrender, but he handled his defeat with dignity, and negotiated favourable terms. The Highlanders burnt the barracks and moved on.

After Culloden, the shattered remnants of Prince Charles's force rallied here under Cluny Macpherson, and awaited the arrival of their Prince. On the 20th April, 1746 a messenger delivered his cold response: 'Let every man seek his safety in the best way he can'. Bitterly disappointed, the dispirited and ragged survivors of the Jacobite army disbanded there and then. So Ruthven, scene of many violent actions in the past, was the setting for the last sad act of the '45. Nowadays it is a peaceful place where cattle graze around the castle mound, and pony trekkers ride across its flanks. The clachan has gone, and the only trace of the old settlement is the solitary building of Ruthven Farm. But so long as the barrack ruins stand, the memories will remain.

Sergeant Molloy stated that the Barrack-wife at Ruthven was a Mrs. Macpherson, and Dr. Douglas Simpson has left us with the following tantalising thought: was she the mother of a famous writer whose remains lie in the Poets Corner of Westminster Abbey? James Macpherson was born at Ruthven in 1738 and he would, no doubt, remember all his life the events he witnessed there as a little boy. He received a good education, and eventually became headmaster of the village school.

In 1762 he published Fingal, a 'translation' from the Gaelic of Ossianic verse which set the literary firmament alight. Further works followed, and Macpherson was lionised, but later there was bitter controversy over provenance. In the 1790's he retired to Badenoch, where he built Balavil house (designed by Robert Adam) and was a well-loved and generous local benefactor.

BLUE HARE

NETHYBRIDGE & ABERNETHY - the Great Wood of Caledon

It is obvious that people have lived about here for ages, and between the B970 and the Spey, by Abernethy Church, the ruined Castle Roy is claimed to be the oldest castle in Scotland. Set on a low mound of glacial till, the four walls enclosed a small courtyard, and there would have been simple lean-to buildings around the court. A small defensive tower is built into the walls by the single entrance. Almost inevitably, it must seem, the 12th Cent. castle is said to have been a stonghold of the 'Wolf of Badenoch', but he is unlikely to have needed a crude shelter such as this so close to his castle at Loch an Eilein.

The Nethy is bridged near to its junction with the Spey, and the village of Nethybridge has grown around the crossing. A charming place of substantial Victorian houses and hotels, it seems to have been created with quiet country holidays in mind. It is often the case in Strathspey that the amenities and attractions are out of all proportion to a village's size, and Nethybridge is typical of this.

The village is a noted fishing centre, and one of the hotels is known to salmon anglers everywhere. All visitors staying in the village have the opportunity to fish the Spey and other local waters. It is possible to swim, and to play tennis, golf and bowls in the village. The locality can be explored on horseback, and it is a perfect setting for walking and bird-watching. Winter sports enthusiasts are well catered for with langlauf in the surrounding woods, and downhill skiing at nearby Cairngorm.

However incredible it may seem today, this quiet and serene

little rural backwater was once the hub of a mighty industrial enterprise. Down the Spey bridge road, between the village and the river, the white harled buildings of the farm at Coulnakyle look inwards and away from the weather. Less than 250 years ago Coulnakyle was leased for the local headquarters of the York Buildings Co., and in the middle of the 18th Cent. the company worked the local forests for timber and charcoal, and they smelted iron ore, brought by pack horses from the mine at Lecht. The iron works were near to the old mill of Balnagowan, down by the river, and, like the rest of the enterprise, they were not a commercial success.

York Buildings, in London, housed a water pumping works, and the company was established to supply water to parts of central London. After the 1715 rebellion they bought up some of the forfeited estates of the defeated Scots as a potentially profitable diversification, and their local operations developed from this landholding. The boom started when they obtained a concession to fell the timber on the Grant estates, and they instigated the practice of floating the timber in huge rafts down to the port at the river's mouth. Many of the ships of Nelson's era, and many of the water pipes in London and elsewhere, were made from Abernethy and Rothiemurchus pine. The operations, which never made a profit for

the company, transformed the appearance and the economy of the area.

The company did have profitable enterprises elsewhere, and the lead mines at Strontian, in Ardnamurchan, had General Wade as an 'Adventurer' in 1728. This man of very many parts actually made money out of his investment, and at one time he lent a considerable sum to the Duke of Atholl.

The Nethy & the Great Wood of Caledon

On the north-eastern slopes of Cairngorm, not far below the summit, Marquis's Well takes its name from the Marquis of Huntly, who is said to have paused here for refreshment whilst pursuing the vanquished Earl of Argyll in 1594. The spring adds its water to the small stream flowing from the declivity of Ciste Mhearad, and snow often lies here far into the summer. The deep and narrow valley of Strath Nethy, which runs north from the watershed by Loch Avon, receives the water from this, and from the many other streams rising in the mountains on either hand. At Bynack Stable, only four miles away, the Nethy is already a river of significant size.

At Bynack the scenery changes, and the mountains seem to simply melt away. The country to the north is an undulating mass of drumlins and general glacial till that makes for an interesting landscape. This was once the bed of a glacial lake, and the low hills were deposited from water flowing under melting ice. They now form a wonderful moorland of heather and other ericaceous plants, with rocky outcrops and many ancient trees. It is a delightful place in which to walk, but the going is always hard. The river flows north across the moor, and in many places it has carved deep and interesting gorges. About two miles beyond Bynack Stable it enters Abernethy Forest, and from there to its confluence with the Spey, it flows through an ancient woodland.

After the last ice age a great boreal forest spread across the northern hemisphere and literally girdled the Earth. Enormous tracts of coniferous woodland still stretch across N. America and Europe, but much of the old forest has disappeared from Britain, a victim of the need for clear ground, and our apparently insatiable demand for softwood.

Most of the large coniferous woodlands in Britain now are artificial, creations of the Forestry Commission and a few private owners, and they tend to consist of close-planted imported species of quick growing trees. Scotland has its share of this type of woodland, and 'tax-avoidance' planting has been rapidly increasing the area that is privately owned. The plantings have often produced a characteristic blanket woodland of spindly and barren trunks rising from an apparently lifeless underburden, and whilst these woodlands may be commercially valuable, they are aesthetically dead.

It is fortunate that Scotland has retained large areas of natural pine forest, which has been the native woodland for the past few thousand years. In a few remnants of the old pine woods it is still possible to get an idea of how the country must have looked before the onset of man. The largest surviving areas are to be found in and about the Strathspey, typically in the forests of Abernethy, Rothiemurchus and Glen More.

Juniper, Scots pine and yew are the only conifers indigenous to Britain, and the old forest remnants consist mainly of native Scots pine and juniper, with thickets of birch and rowans. There is usually some alder and willow scrub in the damper places. The tree spacing varies, but it is nowhere very dense, and old trees usually lie and rot where they have fallen. In many areas the regeneration of the trees seems good, despite the deer, and there is also a large, rich and varied assortment of plants, animals, and insects in a deep and colourful underburden that flourishes only where there is sufficient light.

The Scots pine is a most interesting tree, and is tremendously varied in appearance depending on its age. Young and immature trees are quite undistinguished, with greyish bark, dark green needles and a roughly conical shape. As such there is little to distinguish them from many other conifers. With maturity comes a contrast so great that the old trees might be easily mistaken for a different species.

There is probably no more beautiful and majestic tree than a mature Scots pine, with its new bark shining like freshly etched and beaten copper in the bright sunshine of a spring day. These noble old trees display venerable age in every crack, crease, furrow and wrinkle of their lower trunks. Higher up, the new bark glows beneath broad umbrellas of the darkest green, and the canopies of fragrant pine-needles provide a perfect foil for the yellow pollened spikes of the new cones.

NEWTONMORE - The wildcats' lair

Between Dalwhinnie and Newtonmore the scenery changes as the bleak and stony moors are left behind. The road falls for some 400 feet between the villages, and the descent into Spey Valley after the journey from the south is usually accompanied by a feeling of relief. There is always such a marked contrast between the harsh and windswept exposure of the heights and the comparatively snug and cosy shelter down below. The A9 exit for Newtonmore is at Ralia, where there is a superb information centre close to the road. A specially constructed viewing point commands a splendid vista, and the adjacent exhibition gallery always has something interesting on display.

Some two hundred years ago the Duke of Gordon's new Spey bridge provided a short-cut to the Perth road and cut out the long way round via Laggan. Also about this time, the tenants of the clachans on the Calder were evicted to make way for sheep, and they moved to the growing settlement downstream. So Newtonmore became, literally, the new town on the moor, and it also became an important cattle market. The arrival of the railway in the mid-19th Cent. brought more houses, more residents, more hotels and more visitors. The village rapidly grew into a popular holiday resort, and so it remains today.

Although the village is small, there is plenty to do and see here, and there are some delightful local shops. A particular favourite is an antique and bric-a-brac establishment of the sort that is only a distant memory in the south. If Speyside is a land of contrasts, Newtonmore is a place of extremes. 'Waltzing Waters', just off

Main Street, provides the very latest in spectacular entertainment - a complex presentation combining water, light and sound. Unique in Britain, it is quite indescribable, and really has to be seen. In total contrast, the Clan Macpherson Museum, at the other end of the village, contains some of the most ancient and venerable relics in the area.

The Macphersons, were, of course, until quite recently, the dominant family in the locality, and their seat was Cluny Castle, about 5 miles along the Laggan road. The present building is a charming Victorian fantasy that is a pastiche of many different architectural periods and styles. It was built as a replacement for the original home of Cluny Macpherson, which was destroyed by Cumberland's forces in 1746. Poor Cluny paid a high price for his loyalty to the Jacobite cause, and he was a fugitive in the local hills for ten years. The loyalty of his followers may be judged from the fact that the £1000 reward for his capture was still unclaimed when he finally escaped to France in 1755. He died there, a sad and lonely man, in 1756.

A proud and, at one time, fierce clan, their emblem is a wildcat, and the clan motto is 'Touch not the cat but a glove' ('but', or 'bot', is old Scots for 'without'). The direct line of Macphersons became extinct some 50 years ago, and the castle was sold. Trees now screen it from the common gaze, and it is not open to visitors. Fortunately, at the time of the sale, a committee of clansmen bought many of the most treasured possessions, and these can now be seen in the little museum at the junction of the Perth and Laggan roads.

Amongst the exhibits are the 'magic' Black Chanter - a gift from the fairies, and the 'Green Banner of Clan Chattan' - a guarantee of victory in battle. There are also the sad remains of James Macpherson's fiddle - last played immediately before his unjust execution at Banff in 1700. James was a legendary freebooter, loved by ordinary folk but hated by the authorities. Captured in Keith, he was the last person to be tried under the old system of 'Heritable Jurisdiction', and was sentenced to hang between two and three o'clock in the afternoon. Knowing that a reprieve was on the way, Lord Braco had the town clock put forward by fifteen minutes, and thus ensured Macpherson's demise.

A new clock was once the sign of the growing importance of a town, and when Banff went upmarket the redundant movement came to the Macpherson Museum. The old clock face shows the correct time in Dufftown. There are many other Macpherson memorabilia, some wonderful silver, and interesting exhibits of local history and the development of shinty. The museum is open every day from May to September, and entrance is free.

Before motor vehicles were developed, people walked or rode a garron, or Highland pony. Queen Victoria used this mode of transport quite a lot during her time in the Highlands, and she may well have been the first person to go sight-seeing here on horse back. Ewan Ormiston, a local man, introduced Pony Trekking many years ago, and it is now a popular pastime. Mr. Ormiston's grandson maintains the tradition at Croila Trekking Centre, and the Haflinger Centre operates all the year round from their stables about two miles out of town on the Laggan road. No great skill is needed, and virtually anyone can and will enjoy an outing on these gentle steeds.

Badenoch Angling Association has extensive waters, with fishing in nearby lochs, and in the Spey and other local streams. Resident visitors can purchase permits in the town. The site of the old cattle fairs, down by the river, is now a magnificent 18 hole golf course. Balavil Sport Hotel has a swimming pool, and there are public tennis courts and, for the less energetically inclined, bowling greens in Golf Course Road.

Highland games were another Victorian revival, and the Newtonmore Games and Clan Macpherson gathering take place here at the beginning of August. Visitors outside the three summer months have a great opportunity to watch games of a different sort. Shinty has a long and honourable history, and was popular here more than 100 years ago. The Strathspey teams are recognised as the arch exponents of the game, and Newtonmore has an unequalled record of 28 championship wins. There is an intense rivalry with Kingussie, who also have an impressive record.

This is not merely a summer resort, and winter sports enthusiasts are adequately catered for. Away from the obvious but crowded pistes of Cairngorm, which is not so far away, there is delightful off-piste and langlauf skiing in the Monadhliaths, and the adjacent countryside. And, if the snow fails to materialise, there is a dry slope on the Laggan road.

All lovers of the 'great outdoors' will find this a perfect place for a quiet holiday. Walkers, bird-watchers, botanists, artists and photographers are literally spoilt for choice. Habitats range from the broad expanses of the river flood plain to the innermost recesses of the Monadhliaths, where eagles, wild goats and other rarities are relatively commonplace. And all are within easy walking distance of the town.

SHINTY - Scotland's national sport

'Caman' is a gaelic word that can mean a 'curved stick' or a 'club', and a game of *camanachd ,* or shinty, is a ball game played with camans, which look a bit like hockey sticks. It can be a fast moving, exciting and highly entertaining spectacle and, like golf, which is a truly Scottish game, shinty is really Scotland's national sport. In common with Rugby Union, it is an amateur game that is played for love and not for money.

Administratively, the country is divided into two areas: north and south, with four divisions in each. The mainstays of the sport are the Marine Harvest leagues, and the many other sponsored competitions and cup matches. The season starts on the first Saturday in September and continues into June, and there are three highlights in the shinty year: the Glenmorangie Cup Final, played on a three year cycle at Oban, Fort William, and Inverness; the representative game: North v. South; and the under-21 Grampian Cup. A six-a-side indoor championship is played in the Stakis Aviemore Centre in November.

Shinty is thought to have originated amongst the ancient Celts, who played something like it as a war-game or battle training exercise. Its close affinity with the Irish game of hurling lends credence to its Celtic roots, and there were documentary references to camanachd as early as 1100 AD. Roger Hutchinson, the author of the standard history of the game, quotes many references to shinty in ancient Irish and Scottish literature, where it is often used symbolically as a trigger for violent action. He also postulates a

Norse connection, based on descriptions of a very shinty-like game in the Icelandic sagas of some eight hundred years ago.

The game was being played in Argyll in the 1880's, and the Shinty Association was founded in Kingussie in 1893. But the Strathspey game goes much further back than that. In 18th Cent. Rothiemurchus shinty was an established sport, and Elizabeth Grant, in her *Memoirs of a Highland Lady*, had this to say about an event associated with the Floaters' Ball at Christmas in 1813:

> ... *The amusements began pretty early in the day with a game at "ba", the hockey of the low country, our Scotch substitute for cricket. It is played on a field by two parties, who toss a small ball between them by means of crooked sticks called clubs. The Highlanders are extremely fond of this exciting game, and continue it for hours on a holiday, exhibiting during its progress many feats of agility. There were always crowds of spectators. Our people kept up the game till dark, when all the men - above a hundred - went to dinner in the barn, a beef and some sheep having been killed for them..*

And some say that the modern game is tough!

Nowadays, shinty is a well organised and well managed sport controlled by the Camanachd Association. There are obvious similarities to hockey, and the rules of the modern game seem to owe something to both hockey and Association football. But the similarities should not be pushed too far, for there are many differences, and shinty has fewer and simpler rules, so there are not so many stoppages.

Shinty can field a bigger team of twelve players. The field of play and goals are bigger too: the pitch can be between 140 & 170 yards long and between 70 & 80 yards wide, and the goals are 12 feet wide & 10 feet high. In addition to the referee, there are two goal judges and there may be four linesmen.

Play is often fast and furious, and strangers to the game will be surprised by the overhead play. This can be used to great advantage with the hit-in or shy, roughly equivalent to the footballers' throw-in. In shinty, the player, outside the side line, throws the ball into the air and strikes it with the caman. At the time of contact the ball must be above head height. It is permitted to play and miss, but the hit passes to the other side after two failures.

Shinty players need to be extremely fit. The game is very, very physical, and the pace, vigour and rivalry of the teams seem to constitute all the ingredients for a blood bath. Nothing could be further from the truth, and although no quarter is given or expected, hard but clean play seems to be the rule rather than the exception. The spectators are intensly partisan, extremely vocal and very good natured, and the main invective seems to be reserved for unpopular decisions by the referee - what else are referees for?

The excitement is immediate, gripping and infectious, and in no time at all a visitor will be jumping up and down and cheering and booing with everybody else. After a local game, both teams and many supporters will be off together for a friendly inquest at either the Balavil or the Silverfjord hotels.

Shinty has been maligned in many ways. It has been described by saloon bar wags as a blood sport, as legalised tribal warfare, and as hockey without rules. These sort of comments by Sassenachs, or other ignorant folk, at best raise only a pitying smile in Strathspey, and they do nothing for the reputation of an unusual and ancient sport.

The game is played locally in Kincraig, Kingussie and Newtonmore, and visitors who ignore it deprive themselves of lots of enjoyment. An outing to a shinty match will provide a perfect Saturday afternoon's entertainment if there is no snow, or if the pleasures of the hills and ski slopes pall. There is keen rivalry amongst the local teams, whose supporters can be quite fanatical about the game. They have good reason, too, for Newtonmore and Kingussie are both legendary clubs, and Newtonmore have no less

KINGUSSIE 4 - NEWTONMORE 7   26/9/92

than twenty-eight Championship wins.

The Shinty Year Book, which can be bought locally, is an interesting read for all who have an interest in sport of any kind. It seems that the local teams will have to look to their laurels, for recent championships have been won by Fort William and the Isle of Skye. Oh the shock, the horror, and the shame of it! And have they been getting just a mite complacent in the local villages? Upsets of this sort can do nothing but good for the game, which is now popular in parts of Canada, and is even played in some English schools. Who knows what the future may bring? If the Olympics ever come to Glasgow or Edinburgh, shinty could become an Olympic sport. Now there's a thought.

The Camanachd Association centenary falls in 1993. It will be inaugurated on April 3rd by a commemorative match in period dress between Kingussie and Cowal. There is to be a special book, commemorative medallions, and an interesting programme of exhibitions and special events that will run throughout the year. The Centenary Cup Final is at Fort William on June 5th, and Spey Valley visitors who make the short journey should be well rewarded by a memorable game.

INVERDRUIE, ROTHIEMURCHUS & GLENMORE - woods, water & the eternal hills

The view of the Cairngorms from the village is possibly one of the best things about Aviemore. The panorama of seemingly distant peaks, and the intriguing gap at the beginning of the great pass of the Lairig Ghru, have a permanent appeal. Constantly changing in response to every shift of light, to the time of day, and to the relentless march of the seasons, the spectacle never palls, and the mountains seem to beckon irresistibly.

The most direct way to the hills is along the ski road, which leads from the south end of the village through Inverdruie and Coylumbridge. Inverdruie is an appealing little place with an excellent Visitor Centre (run by the Rothiemurchus Estate), a number of very good shops, and a fish farm.

The Grants of Rothiemurchus are a cadet branch of the great Clan Grant, and the 13th Laird is a direct descendant of the 16th Cent. Chief, John Grant of Freuchie. It is, perhaps, ironic that the junior branch, styled 'Youngers of Rothiemurchus', thrives, whilst the direct line of the Grant chiefs expired long ago. Rothiemurchus is a huge estate of around 20,000 acres, and it comprises just about every type of countryside that could be imagined. There are farms with arable and pasture land, mountains, moorland, bogs, lochs and rivers, and a great and wonderful tract of old Caledonian forest.

This is a large area of natural pine forest, which has been the native woodland for the past few thousand years. In this remnant of the old pine woods it is still possible to get an idea of how the country looked before the onset of man. Much of this old wood of

The place in Inverdruie for excellent food all day, and well into the night!

Teas, coffees and light refreshments during the day and candle-lit *a la carte* dinners, served by attentive waitresses, in the back-room bistro from 6.15 p.m. *Come and sit by the comfort of the woodburning stoves, and enjoy memorable food.*

THE GALLERY
Tel: 0479 810163

Corrour House Hotel
Inverdruie, Aviemore,
Inverness-shire
PH22 1QH.
Scottish Tourist Board,
4 Crowns, Highly Commended

A lovely country house Hotel, set in four acres of secluded garden and woodland, with marvellous views of the Lairig Ghru Pass and the Cairngorm Mountains.

A relaxed and homely atmosphere where country lovers are assured of a warm welcome from mine hosts, David and Sheana Catto.

There are ten spacious bedrooms with all modern facilities, two lounges with cosy log fires and excellent food and wine.

For Brochure and Tariff, phone: (0479) 810220.

Caledon has been worked commercially and no longer truly represents the wild country of long ago, but it does have an oddly primeval feel, and it provides a real flavour of the past.

The simplest way to appreciate this is to go down the road opposite the Visitor Centre and follow the signs to Loch an Eilein. Once there, take the waterside path to the left for a circuit of this most delectable of lochs. The ruined small castle on the island was yet another stronghold of the 'Wolf of Badenoch', and there are plans for its repair and restoration.

The loch has an incomparable setting below the low but steep crags of Ord Ban and Kennapole Hill, whilst to the south-east, the outliers of the Sgorrans provide a fitting backdrop to the majesty of the trees. The rough track undulates and winds through an idyllic woodland, and there is a constant background murmer from the myriad birds, insects, and the breeze. Bird-watchers will have a field day, and uncommon species include crested tit and crossbill. Over by the loch there is always the possibility of a fishing osprey, for this is a favourite haunt of the local birds, and ospreys once nested on the castle on the island.

Many of the pines at the south end of the loch are enormous, and they are obviously very old. Indeed, some of them would have been seedlings at the time of the Jacobite rebellion in 1745. Despite their great age many of the trees are still fertile, and the variety of seedling trees indicates the continued natural regeneration of the forest. Deer are quite fond of young pine shoots, and their grazing is one of the factors that hinders the growth of new trees. Roe are quite numerous here, and the local deer are also relatively big. The path continues round the west side of the loch, back to the Visitor Centre and car park.

Rothiemurchus has much to offer each and every visitor, and there is a network of well maintained footpaths on which visitors are free to wander. The Estate publishes an interesting and useful little guide, which is free. Copies may be obtained from the visitor centres

at Inverdruie and Loch an Eilein, or from many points throughout the estate.

From Inverdruie, the road goes on past the B970 junction to Glenmore and the Cairngorm chair lift. For most of the way there are wonderful views of the Cairngorm range to the south, whilst the road is bounded on the other side by the lower, but much more immediate, Kincardine hills. There are hills, water and woodland all about, and the transition from the glitz of Aviemore is so sudden that it is almost unbelievable.

The great sheet of water that extends to the south is Loch Morlich, which has become a popular holiday resort. There are car parks and picnic spots all along the roadside shore, and the Forestry Enterprise have a popular camp and caravan site in the pine woods at Glenmore. There is a delightful beach.

Glenmore is a tiny and unpretentious hamlet at the NE corner of Loch Morlich. It comprises a Post Office-cum-Cafe-cum-General Store, a Youth Hostel, the Reindeer House, the Forestry Enterprise Visitor centre and a chapel. There is also a group of foresters' houses. In the appropriate seasons the resident population is augmented by the transients at the Youth Hostel, on the caravan/ camp site, and in the few B&B houses. These are often people who came one week for a week and wanted to stay on without really knowing why. They all went home, of course, but only after developing a tendency to come back year after year. It is that sort of place.

By the green here there is a large erratic boulder set in an area of paving. This is the Norwegian Stone, and it is a hallowed memorial to the very many Norwegians of Kompani Linge who lived and trained in this district, and who subsequently died on operations during the last war. It is refreshing to see that some people still care - there are always fresh flowers at the base of the stone. The present Youth Hostel, which was the Operations Centre for the famous Telemark raid, was once a hunting lodge of the Dukes of Richmond and Gordon.

Reindeer are one of the great attractions of Glenmore, and one or two nursing cows are usually corralled by Reindeer House, just opposite the entrance to the caravan site. There is an interesting little shop and exhibition inside the house. Each day, at about 11 a.m. and 2 p.m., Mrs. Smith, one of the the owners, takes a party of visitors to a herd pastured near Glenmore. This is a great excursion, not only for children, for reindeer are delightfully gentle and friendly beasts. They seem to like the company of people, and a brief acquaintance will show why they are beloved by the Lapps.

Reindeer, which are quite unlike red and roe deer, were once widespread in Strathspey. Indigenous long ago, they were hunted to extinction along with the wild boars and the wolves. Mr. Mikel Utse, a Swedish Lapp, visited Aviemore in 1947 and decided that it was reindeer country. He won a long battle against the bureaucrats and introduced the first beasts about 1952. After a series of reverses the animals settled down, and as their numbers increased the main herd roamed freely on the local hills.

Recently there have been problems once again, with 10% of the herd being lost each year. It seems that many of the people on the hills take drinks with them in metal cans. When some people have had their drink they flatten the can and throw it away. A reindeer can lick this up, and the can lodges at the back of the reindeer's throat. It doesn't choke; it simply starves to death. The problem was solved when the main herd was moved away from the tourist area. It is now flourishing again in Glenlivet. What an indictment of our modern way of life!

It may be well to explain that Glen More is the open-ended valley that extends, roughly, some three or four miles from the hamlet of Glenmore to Ryvoan, in the north. It is traversed from end to end by the Thieves Road - the ancient *Rathad nam Mearlach* - and it has the Kincardine hills on one hand and the Cairngorms on the other. It is a very small area of very great beauty, and it is worthy of far more than the cursory interest usually displayed by transients *en-route* to places of larger size and greater renown. There is a lot of pleasant walking on the forest roads, and the countryside here provides a great deal of very good value for very little effort.

Everyone who has come this far ought to go on to Cairngorm, and the chairlift car park is only three miles away up a steep and very scenic road. Not the least important feature of this mountain is its sheer accessibility, and the first chairlift was erected in 1961. Long before that, Cairngorm was the most easily approached of the 4000 ft.+ summits of the Cairngorm hills. True, it is some 9 miles from Aviemore, but there had long been a road of sorts to Glenmore Lodge, and a track beyond there. The favoured way was up the windy ridge of An t'Aonach, and the track may still be found just above Clach Bharraig - the Foundation Stone - the enormous erratic boulder so prominent on the hillside above the start of the one-way system up to the main carpark.

Seen from a reasonable distance, say a mile or so, the N face of Cairngorm is an impressive sight. Close to it is a mess in places, and Coire Cas is an awful mixture of eroded hillside, snow fences, a weird collection of assorted ironmongery, and a service road. It doesn't look too bad in winter and early spring, for snow provides a blanket to hide the wounds, and a multitude of skiers obscures the multiude of devices used to get them up the hill. But the skiing season is short - some may say it is non-existent - and for the rest of the year the flank of the mountain in Coire Cas is a sorry sight. Here, with a vengeance, is vivid proof that distance lends enchantment to the view.

In the context of the mountain the disfigurement is small, and the Chairlift Company do all they can to mitigate the effects of a constant stream of visitors. This includes landscape repair work; and we are all part of the problem. There is also much concern about the effects of people-pressure on the plateau as a whole, and a Government-sponsored working party is studying ways and means of dealing with a potentially very serious problem.

Take some warm clothes, book a return, and go up on the

chairlift to the top station, which is at 3600 ft. After the ride, a relatively easy ascent of 500 ft. on carefully graded granite slabs leads to the summit at 4084 ft.. Westwards, the view passes over the great corries, with their sheer cliffs and lingering snow, then ranges across Loch Morlich to Rothiemurchus, the Monadliaths, and beyond. The Spey valley opens up towards the north from distant Aviemore, and the moors beyond Abernethy stretch away from the foreground bulk of the Kincardine Hills.

Eastwards, the view encompasses the Bynacks, and across the Loch Avon trench - invisible from here because of the contour of the hill - the granite-torred Ben Avon massif lies behind the knobbly bulk of Beinn Mheadhoin. To the south, little Loch Etchachan nestles in the cradle of its surrounding peaks. To the right of the loch the great hump of Ben Macdui dominates the view, and right again from that, the summits of Cairn Toul, Angels Peak and Braeriach all pop up from the far side of the Lairig Ghru. Whatever the season there will be snow fields in view, and the essentially sub-arctic nature of the terrain is clear for all to see. It will be notably cooler than down below.

When seen from the north, which is the aspect open to the roads, the range is steep and craggy, and is mountainous indeed. The new visitor may then be surprised by the southern prospect from the summit of Cairngorm. There are craggy mountains to be seen from here, but they are all quite far away, and the immediate surroundings are more akin to rolling moorland, which is exactly what the Cairngorm plateau is, but because of its altitude and climate, it is tundra, and very interesting to the naturalist.

It will be obvious that little in the way of normal vegetation grows up here, and the ground cover is mainly rough and scarified granite grit bestrewn with sundry boulders. There are patches of vegetation here and there, but they are sparse and frugal, and there is little or no grass. There are just irregular and somewhat crusty cakes, which consist mainly of sedges, club mosses and various lichens. This is a hostile wilderness indeed, and it is an uncomfortable place on a cold grey day with a chilly wind. Most people who come this far have a look at the weather station and the views, take a few photographs, and then go down the way they came up. That is fine, so far as it goes, but Cairngorm offers more than that to the interested visitor.

Follow the faint track down to the west that goes towards the edge of Coire an t-Sneachda, then turn left and go gently downhill into Coire Raibeirt. This is a gathering ground for snow melt water, and an appreciable stream may be followed over an area of peculiar wetland. The ground is soggy but quite firm, and there is only a very thin crust of wet vegetation on the underlying rock. Much of the moss is black, which seems to be typical of mosses that spend much of each year beneath the snow.

As the slope increases cross over to the left and make for the cliff top, following the faint track that ascends from Loch Avon. This position provides a good viewpoint for the massive cliffs at the head of the loch, and it also gives a view of the loch, and of the Shelter Stone. The truncated cone of Shelter Stone Crag dominates the view on the far side, and its two gullies - Castle Gates to the left and Pinnacle to the right - are rarely free from snow. The black peak, towering above the screes to the left of the crag, is Carn Etchachan. It is a striking scene.

Turn left again, and follow the edge up to the rocky eminence of Stac an Fharaidh. There are some dramatic views from here, and the southern prospect is practically as good as that from Cairngorm summit, but with the added bonus of Loch Avon immediately and far below.

Turn back from the summit of the Stac, and carry on contouring round the base of the hill to the north. There is a marked change in vegetation here, and a sparse grass appears, with some trifid rush poking through in the damp patches. Sundry small clumps of moss campion and creeping azalea are dotted about, and the pink flowers add a welcome touch of warm colour in early summer. The study of the lichens and mosses could be a life's work in itself, but very little effort is needed to experience their variety and beauty close-to. As Edwin Waugh once wrote:

Oh the wilderness is my delight
Where the whirring red grouse springs
From his heathery nest in the mountain's breast
With the dew upon his wings.
Wild and free; wild and free;
Where the moorland breezes blow.

The grassy tundra here is home to many ptarmigan, and there is always the chance of an eagle over the loch. When the ski tows appear over the crest of the rise, bear left, and then go downhill to the chairlift. This quiet and gentle walk of three to four miles needs about as many hours if it is to be enjoyed to the full.

Some words of warning: **do not undertake this walk if the weather forecast is not good.** In the warmth of a summer's day the Cairngorm plateau may seem to be a pleasant place. It is, but a thick fog or howling blizzard can come from nowhere at any time and in any season, and in poor visibility it is easy to get lost. Also remember that the chair lift shuts down when wind speeds are high.

STRATHSPEY - MAP & USEFUL INFORMATION

WEATHER REPORTS: 0898 500 424
TOURIST INFORMATION:
Dufftown - 0340 20501, Summer
Grantown on Spey - 0479 2773
Keith - 0542 22634, Summer
Tomintoul - 080 74285, Summer
CLYDESDALE BANK
Aberlour, Dufftown, Rothes
Keith, Tomintoul
BANK OF SCOTLAND
Aberlour, Grantown, Keith
ROYAL BANK OF SCOTLAND
Dufftown, Keith
SCOTTISH TSB
Grantown, Keith
CHEMISTS: Dufftown, Grantown, Keith
EARLY CLOSING:
Aberlour - Wednesday
Archiestown - Thursday
Craigellachie - Thursday
Dufftown - Wednesday

Grantown - Thursday
Rothes - Wednesday
Keith - Wednesday
Tomintoul- Wednesday
DOCTORS:
Dufftown - 0340 20888
Grantown - 0479 2484
Keith - 0542 22735
Tomintoul - 080 74219
DENTISTS:
Grantown - 0479 2107
Keith - 0542 22244

Crossbill

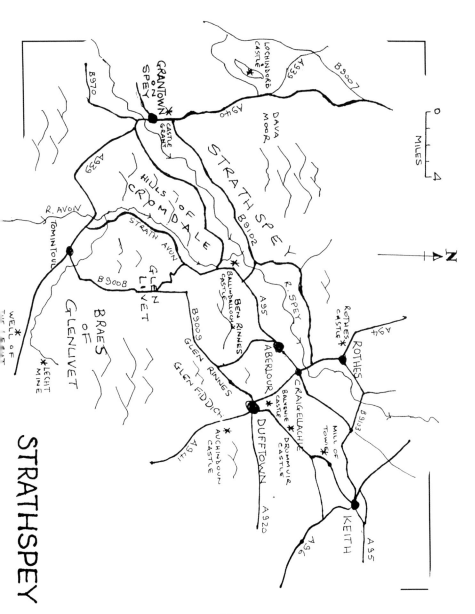

STRATHSPEY

STRATHSPEY - Water, woods and whisky

Downstream from Grantown there is a subtle change in the character of the countryside that has nothing to do with altitude. It is probably a result of different geology, and a deeper and more fertile soil. This is still a hilly country, but these are often rolling hills, and the high mountains look quite far away. Between Grantown and Cromdale, as the road tops a rise, a wonderful vista opens up. The river, wide and deep, and as straight as an arrow flight, cuts through a broad expanse of tree-dappled pasture by the Haughs of Cromdale. Road and river don't always keep close company, and there are some enchanting prospects as the Spey winds its way, in a seemingly endless succession of tortuous bends, through the lush flood plain.

By the riverside here it is easy to understand how the fly-fisherman's Spey cast came into being. This is a method of casting where the line is projected upwards and sideways to spring the rod, and there is no extension to the rear. In so many places on the Spey, a normal back-cast would result in a hopeless entanglement with the trees, so the Spey cast was invented to avoid the problem.

The river does not, of course, flow in splendid isolation, and there are many tributary streams. Roughly midway between Grantown and Aberlour, the Avon adds its pellucid waters to the Spey. Its source is high up in the Cairngorm mountains where the melt waters, fed by the perpetual snow fields below the summit of Ben Macdui, flow down to Loch Avon - one of Britain's highest lochs. For much of its length, the Avon flows through country that is virtually inaccessible to man, and it joins the Spey near to Ballindalloch and the historic Delnashaugh Hotel.

On the banks of the Avon here, the delightful mid-19th Cent. Gothic gatehouse of Ballindalloch Castle looks, for all the world, like something from a tale by the brothers Grimm. Or perhaps it is a refugee from Euro-Disney? Ballindalloch is the ancient seat of the Macpherson-Grants, and has been occupied by the family for some 400 years. The original tower house of the 1540's was progressively extended over a period of some two centuries to produce a castle that easily rivals Blair in its splendour. The castle is now open on Sunday afternoons between May and September. In spring the grounds are a golden carpet of daffodils that would have driven Wordsworth into transports of delight.

There are trees in abundance, and they provide a key to the change in the nature of the landscape. Deciduous trees are now the norm, and the woodlands contain many magnificent stands of alder, sycamore and beech in addition to the almost universal birch. This is not to say that conifers are absent: they are not, and there are many plantations of Scots pine, spruce, fir and larch, but it is the broad-leaved trees that command attention.

The road to Dufftown via Tomintoul seems to have been engineered especially for its views, and there are enchanting prospects of the now distant Cairngorms - an indigo mass, far away across the green, brown and purple variegation of the Glenavon moors. Pity the poor driver who must keep his eyes fixed well and truly on the road. This is an exciting switchback that twists, turns and undulates wildly past the south end of the Hills of Cromdale. There is something of a helter-skelter quality near Bridge of Brown as the road plummets down to the river, and then rises again through a succession of violent hairpin bends.

The main riverside road from Grantown to Aberlour passes by the Bridge of Avon, and this is hill country, too. But the hills are hardly noticed behind their extensive woodland screen. Woodland is a feature, too, of the minor roads through Glen Livet and Strath Avon. Although they all have two lanes, they are often a bit tight in places, but there is very little traffic and there are stunning views of

GATEHOUSE - BALLINDALLOCH CASTLE

the Livet and Avon rivers.

These roads, which are often just green tunnels, seem to run for miles and miles through stunning treescapes of downy birch and bird cherry, with the occasional stand of mountain ash. Not to be confused with the gean, this cherry is a pretty tree, common only in the north. It is a picture in the spring when the pendant racemes, with up to forty white flowers on each one, form a frothy mass of blossom against the soft green background of the leaves. In the autumn, the dying leaves of all these trees harmonise beautifully in glorious red and yellow tints.

The accent of Strathspey is on variety, and it applies both to the country and the towns. This is the most densely populated of all the straths in Scotland, yet the towns and villages never obtrude. They are merely welcome punctuations in and around a great river valley, and there is always a sense of being in the country and of the mountains. It is easy to see why Strathspey has such a broad appeal.

SNIPE

ABERLOUR - shortbread & old shops

Charlestown-of-Aberlour, as it should properly be called, was founded by Charles Grant of Elchies in 1812, and is a quiet village typical of its period and its place. Built directly on the A95 road from Grantown to Banff, there is a long street of pink granite houses standing all of a piece in their Georgian elegance, and as solid as the rock from which they are built. The approach from the south is lightened by the church towers, one on each side of the road, and the village has an air of quiet charm. It has been said many times that good things come in little packages, and this is obvious here. There is a wealth of attractions that would be the envy of many a bigger place.

Particular noteworthy is 'The Village Store', on the High Street at The Square. In a setting that is a model for its period, there is a display of articles and artifacts that would have been for sale at some time in some local shop somewhere during the first fifty years of this century. It is the essence and epitome of all the village stores that have ever been, and should by no means be missed. An associated shop sells modern quality craft ware. The Visitor Centre, also on High Street, has an exhibition illustrating the history of the area.

Alice Littler Park, on the site of the old railway station by the river, commemorates the wife of a local benefactor who was the owner of what was, once, a famous orphanage. The Speyside Way long distance footpath uses the old rail bed here, and the elegant buildings of the old station, all pink and grey granite and white harl, now house tea rooms and various other enterprises. What was once the station platform is now a terrace, and it looks across to the river over an expanse of grass laid out for pitch and put. Nowhere in Speyside is far removed from golf. The elegant suspension foot-bridge a little way down stream replaced a 19th Cent. ferry, and there is a feeling that not much has changed here since then.

The quiet is deceptive because this is a busy place, and Walkers, renowned for their oatcakes and shortbread, have their headquarters here. This is also a whisky town, and Aberlour Glenlivet is nearby. Although not officially on 'The Whisky Trail', the distillery is open to visitors on week days.

Of the many other attractions in and about this attractive town mention must be made of Inveravon Kirk, on the Grantown road, which has a number of Pictish stones. Not too far away, Ballindalloch Castle, by the Bridge of Avon on the Grantown road, is open on Sunday afternoons in the summer.

Lovers of deer, both on the hoof and in the form of venison, should visit Speyside Venison at Balnakyle, just off the Grantown road. Good whisky needs good water, and the Spey and Avon are both nearby. Fishing for resident visitors is available on both rivers, which carry sea and brown trout as well as salmon.

Pony Trekkers are catered for at Aberlour House, and there is a swimming pool at Speyside High school. Surprisingly, there is no golf course in the town, but there is a course at Dufftown, and a good putting green by the river in Alice Littler Park.

Walkers are not neglected, and the 1800 foot summit of Little Conval, crowned by an Iron Age hill fort, can be reached via a track that runs eastwards by the Wood of Allachie behind the town. Near to the distillery, at the southern entrance to the town, a path runs through the woods to the pretty Linn falls on the Burn of Aberlour.

CRAIGELLACHIE - legendary fishing & the last iron bridge

Craigellachie is a name that will evoke an instant response from any salmon fisherman - probably of longing and despair. The village's glory is a world-renowned stretch of the Spey, and a world-renowned hotel, where wealthy fishermen are rumoured to book-in their children at birth for the privilege of fishing certain beats on certain weeks of the year. It probably isn't quite like that in fact, but good fishing has to be reserved a very long time ahead.

Originally there was a coaching inn here, then a new hotel was built to serve the stations when the railways came in the 19th Cent. The railways have now gone, but the hotel remains and it offers 20th Cent. comfort with an aura of Victorian elegance. Fishing is not the only sport catered for, since golf and riding can be enjoyed locally and, in due season, there is stalking to be had.

The hotel looks out onto another local glory: the bridge built by Thomas Telford, maker of the Caledonian Canal. The last cast-iron bridge to be built in Scotland, it was erected in 1814 by a Shrewsbury firm, using local stone married to iron work from Plas Kynaston, near Ruabon in North Wales. The mind boggles at the thought of the problems to be surmounted when bringing the iron work here. The bridge was restored and then by-passed by a new bridge some years ago, and it stands as a picturesque and fitting memorial to one of the civil engineering giants of the past.

A little way downstream from the bridge the Fiddich joins the Spey, and the Speyside Cooperage has a visitor centre on the Dufftown road. This working barrel manufactory offers a unique

TELFORD'S BRIDGE — CRAIGELLACHIE

opportunity to find out all about another important ingredient in the making of Scotch whisky. And here is an interesting fact to titillate the taste buds: the Scots are noted for their thrift, and do not readily throw useful things away. So no one should be surprised to learn that spent whisky barrels are reduced to shavings, which are then burnt in the smoke-houses where smoked salmon is made.

Walkers will be interested in the Speyside Way Visitor Centre, just outside the village on B9015. In addition to details of the Way, the centre can provide detailed information about much else of interest in the locality.

The BURGHEAD BULL

DUFFTOWN - Whisky capital of the world

This is yet another small town created in the Highlands by an enlightened landowner. At the beginning of the 19th Cent. James Duff, the Earl of Fife, built Dufftown as a woollen manufacturing town to provide employment and ease the misery of the local population towards the end of the Napoleonic wars. Although it is a quiet little place, there is no shortage of hotels and restaurants. The central Clock Tower, which dates from late-Georgian times, has been variously the local gaol and then the Town Hall. It now houses an interesting little museum, and serves as a tourist information centre during the summer months.

Nowadays this little town, on the minor road from Keith to Tomintoul, must be regarded as the whisky capital of the world. Built hard by the confluence of the Fiddich and Dullan Water, there are no less than seven malt whisky distilleries nearby.

Glenfiddich is distilled and bottled just off the A941 Elgin road on the northern outskirts of the town. Dating from the 1880's, it must be regarded as a relatively new distillery, but it may fairly claim to have started the modern fashion for drinking single malts. It is also the only Highland distillery to bottle its own whisky on the premises. The distillery is open to visitors every day, except for a short break over the Christmas period.

Down by the river, near to the Mortlach distillery, Mortlach Church stands on a site that has a long and venerable history. The present church has some 14th Cent. bits, but it is generally a modern rebuilding on an ancient foundation. The church does look old, but most of the structure goes back only some 60 years or so. The main glories are in the churchyard, and a tradition that the foundation dates from 566 A.D. is given credence by an intriguing Pictish cross. There are other monuments of the 15th and 16th Cents., and there is a Pictish symbol stone in the porch.

To the north of the town, between the Glenfiddich distillery and the river, the venerable ruins of Balvenie Castle are a reminder of turbulent times gone by. Dating back to the 13th Cent., the castle has had a colourful history and many distinguished residents. King Edward I was an early occupant, and in 1562 it housed Mary, Queen of Scots when she was campaigning against the too-powerful family of the Gordons. There was action here in 1644, and the Jacobites captured it in 1689 after the battle of Killicrankie. Its last occupants were the troops of Butcher Cumberland, during the rebellion of 1745/6.

In the last 200 years it has fallen into disrepair, but it remains impressive in its ruined state. The great yett at the entrance is original, and it needs little imagination to picture this impressive fortress in its prime. The castle is open to visitors from April to September.

There is no lack of things to do, and in addition to some pleasant walking round about, there is golf - 18 holes, at Glenrinnes on B9009. Fishing, on the rivers Dullan and Fiddich - Permits from TV Services & Rutherfords. Tennis - All weather courts in Mount Street.

Keen walkers holidaying in the area ought to climb Ben Rinnes, and it is probably best approached from the hill road of Glack Harness, which runs north-westwards from B9009 about four miles south of Dufftown. Glack Harness runs through a deep declivity between Meikle Conval and Round Hill. Just beyond Glack House, and before entering the valley, start across and up the moor to the west. Make for the obvious knoll of Roy's Hill, and from there walk straight up to the grand granite summit of the mountain. In clear weather there are superb views.

THE WHISKY TRAIL AND RIVERS OF SCOTCH

To many people in many places Speyside is synonymous with whisky, and, in particular, with perhaps the finest malt whiskies in the world. Strathspey is the heartland of Highland Malts, and near to the confluences of the Spey, the Avon, and the Livet the distilleries lie thickly on the ground. This is no accidental location, for most of the ingredients are locally produced, and the all-important Speyside water occurs nowhere else.

The distilling of spirits is an art, the origins of which are lost in the dim and distant mists of time. There is a record from the 1490's which refers to 'eight bolls of malt' required for the making of *aqua vitae*, but the art of distilling the precious spirit would be far older than that. Pennant, writing in the 18th Cent., mentions a Pictish brew that was ale with added heather tops, so beer was a very early drink, and a distillate of this would have been a kind of whisky.

If the origins are obscure, a lot is known of its subsequent chequered history. Whisky of sorts was a common medieval tipple, although during The Auld Alliance, the gentry imported French wines in large quantities up to the 17th Cent. One sad result of James I/VI's accession to the English throne in 1603 was a ban on the importation of claret, which probably increased further the production and consumption of whisky.

Unable to miss the chance of more fat profits, the Government tax on whisky was regularly increased, which caused all sorts of problems. In 1780 the tax on wines was also raised substantially, which again boosted the already heavy demand for illicit spirit. The

WHISKY STILLS

troubles multiplied, and in 1814, in an incredible act of bureaucratic stupidity, all stills of less than 500 gallons were banned. This made good whisky contraband, for only 'rot-gut' came out of the large legal stills, and good quality whisky came only from the small distilleries.

Even King George IV was a drinker of illegal Glenlivet, but was unable to obtain a supply of his favourite when in Edinburgh in 1822. Elizabeth Grant, in her *Memoirs,* tells of her displeasure when commanded by her father to send down to Holyrood the best whisky from the Rothiemurchus cellar. But she emptied her pet bin of aged whisky with the true contraband taste, and it repaired the family's fortunes. The Laird's initiative in Edinburgh was well rewarded, and in due course he received a knighthood and an appointment as a judge in India.

A further Act of Parliament, in 1823, effectively ended the era of illicit distilling and smuggling, and George Smith, the producer of the King's Glenlivet, was the first small producer to go 'legal'. A determined and resolute man, he survived sustained opposition from his former associates, and then opened a large new distillery in 1858. Success brought imitators and a glut of other 'Glenlivet' brands, until in 1880 the firm gained the sole right to the name 'The Glenlivet'.

The whisky made by George Smith and the other distilleries on Speyside was what we today call 'Malt'. The relatively small scale of its production meant that supplies were always limited, and vastly increased demand resulted in the familiar blended Scotch. This contains, perhaps, 50% of malts mixed with grain whisky, which is produced in vast quantities from fermented maize or other grain.

Benjamin Franklin wrote in 1789 that "*...in this world nothing can be said to be certain, except death and taxes*"; to which every whisky distiller will say 'Amen'. But despite the ever increasing imposts of the world's tax gatherers (some things never change) the demand for whisky grows, and there is an enormous market abroad. The drinking of single malts is in fashion again, which is good for the Speyside economy. It is also good for the visitors, who have a unique opportunity to savour the many different and distinctive products of the local firms.

THE MAKING OF THE MALTS

The making of whisky is an art, a craft, a science and a mystery. Superficially, the process is fairly simple: the first stage is a bit like fermenting strong ale, but don't ever say that in a distillery, or you might end up in a mash tun. The process has five stages: malting, mashing, fermenting, distilling, maturing.

MALTING - Barley steeped in Speyside water is spread out on the malting floor to germinate. The barley is regularly turned to avoid over-heating, and after a week or so most of the starch in the grains will have turned into sugar: it is a bit like sprouting beans. The sprouted barley is **malt**, which then goes into the kiln.

Although not hot enough to actually toast the malt, the heat stops the germination, and smoke from the kiln fire adds a distinctive flavour to the malt. On Speyside the kilns are usually fired with peat, but other substances can be used. In the Islands, for instance, seaweed is sometimes added to the flames, and the iodine in this accounts for the somewhat medicinal tang of certain Island malts.

MASHING - The sprouts are stripped off and sent to be turned into cattle food, and the dried malt is passed through a mill, which grinds it into **grist**. Hot water is added (that important element again, unique to each distillery) and the mash is agitated for about a day to turn the malty gruel into **wort**. The liquid is taken off, and the residual grains also go for cattle food - lucky cattle.

FERMENTATION - The cooled wort goes into enormous vats or **wash-backs**. Yeast is added to start off a two to three day fermentation that produces about 5% alcohol in the wort.

DISTILLATION - This two-stage process utilises enormous copper **pots** or stills. Shaped something like onions with bent stems, the first, or **wash still**, has the wort pumped in, and it is then heated near to boiling point. The alcohols vapourise and pass through the stem into a **worm**, which is a water cooled copper coil. The cooling condenses the alcohol, which runs from the worm into the second pot, called the **spirit still**.

The spirit flowing from the wash still is called **low wines**, and these are distilled again from the spirit still. The beginning and the end of the **run** from this still's worm go back for re-distillation, the middle portion, or **middle cut** passes through the **spirit safe**, which is a brass-bound glass box, sealed by the Excise man. The distillation is controlled by the **Stillman**, who can see, but cannot sniff or taste, and he does everything by sight and experience alone.

Distillation is where the mystery and the art come in, and many of the things that happen here cannot be measured, analysed or explained: not even by the stillmen. For example, the shape of the pot influences the taste of the whisky, and when a replacement is needed it has to replicate the old pot exactly. And that means down to the last dent and crease. If it does not, the whisky's character changes.

A wholesaler's rep. talks of one of the firms in Strathisla, that needed to increase output, and built a new distillery. It is an exact replica of the distillery on the opposite side of the river, but the whisky it produces is significantly different to that from the original on the other side. Explain that.

MATURATION - The whisky from the receiver is piped into oak casks in the **bonded warehouse**. Some are new, and some are old sherry casks. It from the casks that the golden colour comes. The spirit lies maturing for eight years or more, and about 2% is lost by evaporation each year. During the maturing subtle changes take place, and some of the alcohol is changed into quite exotic compounds. They all add character to the malt whisky, and they all enhance the smoothness and reduce the bite. Finally, the whisky is diluted to marketable strength with the always important local water, and is bottled ready for sale. It should be noted that whisky does not mature or age in bottles.

The end product is as varied as the distilleries' locations, and they all have their own characteristics and devotees. It should also be noted that in Scotland it is not usual to ask for 'Scotch'. The locals always have a 'whisky'. Finally, there is a plant with a fondness for malt. It is a little black lichen that grows on the outside of bonded warehouse walls. This is the big give-away, and it is always easy to see where whisky is being stored. Brick, concrete or local stone, it really doesn't matter: the black mottle tells the tale.

THE WHISKY TRAIL

This is the age of The Trail, and there are nature trails, woodland trails, heritage trails, castle trails, Mary Queen of Scots, Queen Victoria and Robert Adam trails, and so on, *ad nauseum*. One of the least dotty and most interesting and rewarding of them all is the Whisky Trail. And it is unique.

The distillers don't waste money on TV advertising; they spend it in a far more sensible and creative way. They ask the actual and potential customers to come to the distilleries to see the whisky being made, to learn about its history, and to taste it. This is the idea behind The Whisky Trail; it is brilliant marketing, and it works. Cardhu, Glenfarclas, Glenfiddich, Glen Grant, The Glenlivet, Strathisla, Tamdhu, and Tamnavulin - Glenlivet are the eight distilleries on the trail, which covers about 70 miles of beautiful Speyside roads. Common to them all are a guided tour, a whisky shop, an exhibition and a free dram.

They all have their own particular *cachet,* and at Glenfarclas, for instance, tastings are in the elegant '30's ambience of a ship's saloon, with a delicately plastered ceiling, and oak panelled walls rescued from the great ocean liner *The Empress of Australia.* At Strathisla, the distillery occupies a picturesque old building that dates back to the days of the illicit stills. In total contrast, at Tamdhu, visitors are received in the delightful buildings of the old Knockando railway station, and they also have on show the world's oldest bottle of whisky.

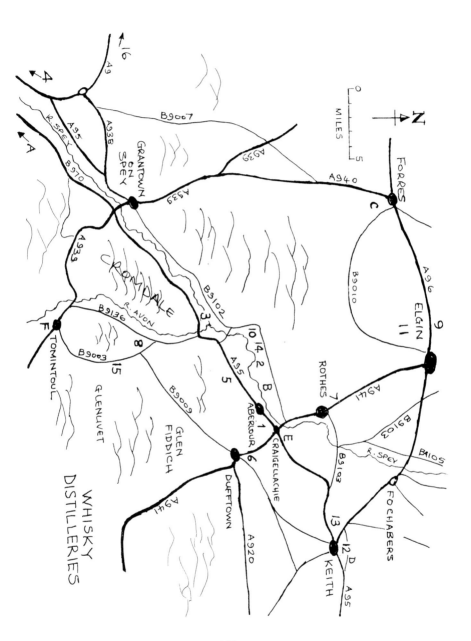

WHISKY DISTILLERIES

So the trail offers more than just a free tipple. It provides two days of interesting and enjoyable excursions for at least two people, one of whom - poor soul - is the abstaining driver. The trail will satisfy and tax the most dedicated *afficianados* of malt whisky. Convenient starting points are Grantown, Tomintoul and Keith, but the trail is well sign-posted by the AA, and the route is shown on the map on the previous page. As an alternative, Highlander Tours run an inexpensive daily excursion from Aviemore.

Eight distilleries comprise the Trail, but more are open to the public. A personal trail can be created from the following list.

WHISKY DISTILLERIES OPEN TO VISITORS

The following distilleries, not all on The Whisky Trail, welcome visitors, usually without appointment. Large parties will need to make a telephone booking in advance. The identifying number or letter identifies the establishment on the map. All these distilleries are open from Monday to Friday between Easter and the end of September, usually between the hours of 10 am to 4 pm. In high summer some may be open longer. An asterisk (*) indicates a distillery that is open all year.

1 **Aberlour**, Charlestown of Aberlour - 0340 5204 *

2 **Cardhu**, Knockando, by Aberlour - 0340 6204 *

3 **Cragganmore**, Ballindalloch - 08072 202 *

4 **Dalwhinnie**, Dalwhinnie - 05282 208 * In the village, off A9.

NOT ON THE MAP HERE.

5 **Glenfarclas**, Ballindalloch - 08072 245 or 247 *

6 **Glenfiddich**, Dufftown - 0340 20373 *

7 **Glen Grant**, Rothes - 03403 413

8 **The Glenlivet**, Ballindalloch - 08073 427

9 **Glenmoray**, Elgin - 0343 542477

10 **Knockando**, Knockando, by Aberlour - 03406 205

11 **Milton Duff**, Nr. Elgin - 0343 54733

12 **Strathisla**, Keith - 05422 7471

13 **Strathmill**, Fife-Keith. **By appointment only** - 05422 2295

14 **Tamdhu**, Knockando, by Aberlour - 03406 221

15 **Tamnavulin-Glenlivet**, Tamnavulin - 08073 442

16 **Tomatin**, Tomatin - 08082 234 In the village, just off A9, between Carrbridge and Inverness. Not on the map above.

RELATED ATTRACTIONS

A. **Cairngorm Whisky Centre**, Inverdruie, Aviemore - 0479 810574 * One of the largest selections of malt whiskies anywhere, with a whisky museum, video theatre, tasting room and shop.

B. **Creative Cask Co.**, Tomlea, Carron - 03406 273 *
Garden furniture manufacture from whisky casks.

C. **Dallas Dhu Distillery**, Nr. Forres
No longer working, and now a comprehensive whisky industry museum - admission charge.

D. **Keith Whisky Barrel Co-operative**, Keith - 05422 7083 *
See the manufacture of garden furniture and other articles from whisky casks.

E. **Speyside Cooperage**, Craigellachie - 0340 881264 *
Working cooperage on the Dufftown road, with an exhibition Viewing gallery to watch coopers at work in the factory.

F. **The Whisky Castle**, Main Street, Tomintoul - 08074 213 *
Its claim to stock the greatest range of whiskies in the Highlands might be contested by the firm at Inverdruie. But there is no doubt that the range is vast, and there are tastings.

GRANTOWN ON SPEY - the head & heart of Speyside

The town's origins go back to 1765, when Sir Ludovic Grant and Mr Grant of Grant advertised in the Aberdeen Journal their proposal for a town. Their prospectus was a mixture of hyperbole, exaggeration and downright untruth that would attract the admiration of a modern estate agent and a summons from the local Trading Standards Officer. The town was to be built close to the Spey and the Abernethy woodlands, about a mile south of Castle Grant, and the offer attracted plenty of attention.

Nicely situated, midway between Blair Atholl and Inverness, midway between the river's source and the sea, and at the junction of important roads, the site had much to recommend it. It had a pleasant climate, decent soil, good air and a good water supply. There were also adequate supplies of fuel and excellent building materials close at hand. It seemed to have all the ingredients for success, and it very nearly failed.

As was usual at that time, it was advertised as a textile manufacturing town. Carefully nursed by Sir James Grant, the industry eventually became established and even flourished for a while. By the beginning of the 19th Cent. a combination of cheap cottons, and the industrial revolution in the south effectively killed off the textiles, but the town had by then become the commercial centre of the area, and it survived.

The railways brought tourists, a change of direction, and a wave of new prosperity. Queen Victoria came in 1860 and liked it, although she made some accurate, if disparaging, remarks about

Castle Grant, which she likened to a factory. The Victorian era saw Grantown become a major resort. Although the railways have now gone, nothing else seems to have altered much since then. It retains a definite, slightly bustling, and rather engaging Victorian air, and it remains deservedly popular.

Visitors usually are attracted at first sight, for this is a charming town, and some parts of it are extremely elegant. The main street is wide and spacious, and the many houses, hotels and shops tend to be imposing and even stately granite buildings. The Square, with its greens and trees, has a pronounced air of elegance, and it is definitely a place in which to sit at ease, mopping up the sunshine.

There is plenty to do here, and there are all the amenities expected in a holiday resort, incuding badminton, bowling and tennis. The Golf Club welcomes visitors, and equipment can be hired. Grantown is a winter sports centre, and curling is an added attraction in the winter. Fishermen need no introduction to the Spey, one of the world's great salmon rivers, and resident visitors have access to excellent fishing on the town water. The many hotels provide a wealth of live entertainments, and a group or a celidh can be heard somewhere or other almost every night.

The southern outlook from the town embraces the Cairngorms, and these will, inevitably, attract keen walkers. But the local woodlands should not be spurned, and there is much interesting and attractive walking country in the vicinity of the town. It may also come as a surprise to learn that roe deer, red squirrels and pine martens are all resident within a few minutes walk of the town centre, and the woodlands between the town and the river contain many unusual plants and birds.

Castle Grant, about a mile north of the town, was once the home of the Earls of Seafield. Originally a 15th Cent. tower house, it was progressively enlarged and extended over the centuries. It was then allowed to become rather decrepit, but it is now being restored by a new owner. The castle, which has many Adam features, may

soon be open again during the summer months.

There is no town museum as such, but the Grantown Heritage Trust has an exhibition in the Courthouse during the summer.

KEITH - Three villages & one town

Nestling in a delightful river valley at the extreme northern edge of the Grampians, this is a prosperous little place, with a population of about 5000 happy people. Keith is a sizeable town by Speyside standards, and it is, in fact, not one town but three. The original settlement, on the east bank of the Isla, is very old, and the remnants are clustered around The Auld Brig - a pretty and very early 17th Cent. high-arched packhorse bridge - at the bottom of Regent Street. The first major expansion started in 1750, only a few years after Culloden, and New Keith, immediately to the east of the old town, is an early Georgian planned town. Fife-Keith, on the opposite bank of the river, was started by the Earl of Fife in 1817.

Keith is a super little town that lacks only an obvious town centre. This is probably a result of the way the town was developed, and the shopping area, around Mid Street, is not at all obvious to the casual visitor. There is a wealth of hotels, pubs. and restaurants, and plenty of parking in both New Keith and Fife-Keith. Early closing is on Wednesday, and there is an indoor market every Saturday in St. Thomas's Hall.

As one would expect, Keith is another whisky town, and the air is often rich with the delicious smell of malting barley. Strathisla is the local malt. This is one of the oldest distilleries in the Highlands, and it has been operating for over 200 years. Incredibly picturesque, it welcomes visitors on week-days between Easter and September.

Whisky is only part of the story here and, in addition to the whisky, woollens are manufactured in the local mills. The town was the commercial capital of Banffshire, and is the centre for one of the greatest agricultural and cattle raising areas of the north. Keith Show - a gigantic agricultural show held every August - is an enjoyable reflection of this interest.

For golfers, there is an 18 hole course in Fife-Keith. There is a swimming pool in Banff Road, and tennis courts in St Rufus Park. There is loch fishing at Loch Park, Drummuir, and free trout fishing in the River Isla, Grange.

Further afield, at the foot of the Hill of Towie, about 3 miles south-west of Keith on the B9014 Dufftown road, the Mill of Towie is a pleasant surprise. It is the estate mill for Drummuir Castle, and this cluster of no-nonsense grey stone buildings is an incredible time-capsule of Victorian industry and ingenuity. This is a working water mill grinding oats to produce various grades of oatmeal, which can be bought at the adjacent shop. Here oats are dried over the kiln, and then stone-ground by a process that has remained unchanged for hundreds of years.

This mill dates from the 19th Cent., but there has been a mill on the site for some 400 years, and water power is still used because it works so well. The produce is 'organic' because that is the way it has always been grown on the estate. There are no gimmicks, it is all quite genuine, and the 1890-something Factories Acts, pasted to the mellow pine planking of a meal chute, are there because no one has yet got round to removing them. Of course there have been changes, and the Granary is now a café serving delicious food, much of it grown on the estate. There is also a good craft shop in the mill.

In a beautiful wooded valley, about 3 miles further along the Dufftown road from the mill, Drummuir Castle - a fantastic Victorian Gothic extravaganza - is the family seat of the Gordon MacDuffs.

On Sundays, from May to September, the castle is open for guided tours, and this is also the home of the MacDuff Clan Centre. Just past the castle, down a winding track, the old walled kitchen garden is well worth a visit. It is open on Sunday, Wednesday, Thursday & Friday afternoons.

ROTHES - Between the mountains and the plains

Straggling along the east bank of the river, and nestling beneath a low arc of protecting hills, the little town of Rothes looks across the Spey to the minor eminence of Ben Aigan. Conceived originally as a crofting village during the great spate of 18th Cent. reconstruction, the inhabitants later turned their attention to alcohol.

There are now many distilleries here, the chief of which, and the most famous, being Glen Grant. The other source of employment is the huge factory on the Garmouth road, at the north end of the town, which converts the abundant spent grain from the many local distilleries into cattle food - alcoholic cows?

There was an agricultural community hereabouts long before the building of the town, and Rothes castle was used by Edward I at the end of the 13th Cent. Once a stronghold of the Leslies, they sold out and moved to Fife in 1700, and the castle was destroyed before the present town was built. Much of the stone was used to make the local houses, and now only a length of broken wall remains, high above the road at the southern entry to the town.

On the far bank of the river, in a splendid setting in the open country, to the right of the road between Rothes and Boat of Brigg, yet another castle ruin bears witness to the turbulent days of old, and is almost a counterpart to Auchindoun.

Without doubt, the main attraction in the town is the Glen Grant distillery. It was built in 1840 by the brothers James and John, whose portraits still grace the bottle labels. The austere and strictly functional lines of the grey stone buildings are relieved only by crow-stepped gables, and the far from fancy turrets of the office block. There is a touch of colour, though, in the bright red paintwork of the doors and the glittering golden cockerels at the gates.

The main attractions are inside, and there is an extremely well-presented tour. Opinions will vary, but the still house is probably the most picturesque place of all. Here there are no less than eight gigantic copper pot stills, each one a different shape and size. It is a sobering thought (no pun intended) that over one million gallons of whisky are produced here each year. All the water used is abstracted from the Caperdonich burn, a little tributary of the Spey, that rises from a spring on the hill behind the distillery.

Anything but a holiday metropolis, this quiet little Speyside town, with its few hotels and shops, welcomes visitors with the mixture of quiet friendliness and reserve that is so typical of the Highlands. This is one of the features that makes Rothes such an attractive place, and there is a surprising number of things to do here. The Recreation Park offers bowls and tennis, and there is a childrens' play area, too. There is golf on the charming little 9 hole course at Blackhill, to the east of the town, and pony trekkers are catered for at Drumbain, just out of town on the Elgin road.

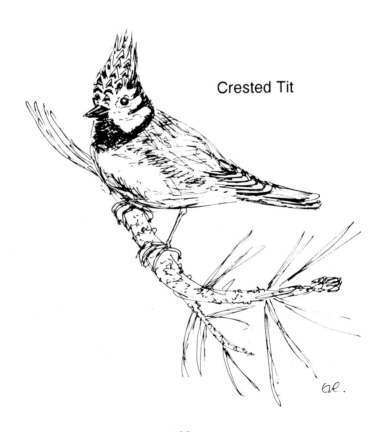

Crested Tit

TOMINTOUL - capital of Avonside

The great military road, planned by Wade to run from Blairgowrie to Fort George, was actually made by General Caulfield. In 1754 the stretch from Well of the Lecht to Grantown was completed by troops of the 33rd. Regiment, under the command of Lord Charles Hay. Some twenty years later it was in regular use as a public road. The old pack-horse track from Nethybridge joined the road a few miles north of the iron-stone mine down by the Well of the Lecht. Near to this junction, and not far from the little clachan of St. Bridget, the 4th Duke of Gordon founded Tomintoul.

The Duke intended that Tomintoul should become a linen manufacturing town. There seemed to be something of an obsession with that particular industry in those days but, at this altitude, the growing season is very short, and the climate is probably too extreme for successful flax crops. There must also have been a lot of competition from other, more favourably placed towns also founded with that intention, so it is not surprising that the industry never really became established. Queen Victoria passed through on a wet and misty day in 1860, and thought it was ...*a most tumble-down poor looking place.* Seven years later, coming up from the Lecht, she remarked that it ..*lies very prettily amongst the trees, hills and fields*...Still prettily located, but now not remotely tumble-down, Tomintoul is still far from being the pulsating hub of the Universe. In an enviable location in the middle of Strath Avon, it is the only centre of population on the river, and this isolation, which was such an impediment in the past, is now one of Tomintoul's most appealing features.

A··D 1754

FIVE · COMPANES
ꝧE · 33ᵈ · REGMENT
RIGHT · HONᵇˡᵉ · LORD
CHAˢ · HAY · COLONEL
MADE ꝧE ROAD · FROM
ꝧERE · TO · ꝧE
SPEY

ꝧE WELL OF ꝧE LECHT

-122-

The Tourist Information Centre, in the Square, has a splendid
exhibition of items relating to the village and the locality. It is one of
the first places to visit. There are some good craft shops and a
remarkable whisky centre, and the village also has an incredible
village store that seems to stock just about everything from buttons to
baguettes.

There are so many other attractions that it could easily have
become another Aviemore, but it escaped that fate and it is still a
quiet and peaceful little place, popular with many discerning lovers
of the outdoors, who use it as a base for their various activities. Hill
walkers and bird watchers have a vast expanse of hill and moorland
at their feet. The Crown Estates of the Braes of Glenlivet stretch
away to the north-east, whilst the wild, lonely and austerely beautiful
country of Glen Avon lies to the south and west. The resort is also
popular as a centre for pony trekking. Tomintoul's close proximity to
the Lecht ski grounds have made it a popular winter sports centre.
There is enjoyable fishing in the Avon and Conglas.

The Avon is a lonely river, flowing from a high and isolated
loch fed by melt waters from the virtually permanent snowfields of
the Cairngorm plateau. The source has a highly dramatic setting in a

rocky amphitheatre beneath the craggy north face of Ben Macdui. The river then flows for a short distance through the Loch Avon Trench - a noted glacial feature - where the ice has scoured a deep and narrow canyon through the granite. The rest of its course is something of an anti-climax, and scenic grandeur compensates for the lack of drama. For most of its forty mile journey to the Spey, the river flows through a wild and empty countryside; empty of buildings and people, that is, for there is an abundance of wildlife in Strath Avon.

The Avon is noted for the purity of its water, which no doubt influenced George Smith when, in 1850, he took over the distillery at Delnabo, by the confluence of the Avon and Ailnack, as an adjunct to his operations in Glenlivet. He produced 'Cairngorm' whisky at Delnabo, and the name must have been derived from the source of

the water, for the mountains of that name are about fifteen miles to the south west. The distillery, which was very small, closed in 1858 after new premises were built in Glenlivet. There is no trace of the distillery now

The Glenlivet Estate was acquired by the Crown some sixty years ago. An enormous and varied tract of country, it contains high mountains, heather moors, woodlands, and many farms. With an area of some sixty square miles, the estate generates an appreciable income from farming and forestry. More income is derived from grouse shooting, deer stalking and fishing, but there is extensive public access too. The Speyside Way runs plumb through the middle, from Hill of Deskie to Tomintoul, and a network of signposted tracks and paths covers the country on either side. A useful free leaflet can be had from the Tourist Information Centre.

This is an area of great beauty that has not yet been 'discovered', and where it is easy to escape from the crowds. There is the sort of quiet and pleasant solitude that is often only a distant memory in the Cairngorms. The remoteness was a major factor in the decision to move most of the Cairngorm reindeers here, for they had a high mortality in Glenmore due to their tendency to lick-up the litter left by tourists. About a dozen animals were lost each year, starved to death by the empty cans lodged in their throats. The herd is thriving in Glenlivet, and the quality has improved as a result of better pasture.

The Tomintoul Country Walk is a three-mile circuit on tracks and country roads that provides a lot of pleasure for little effort. It starts from the car park, about a mile south-west of Tomintoul on the minor road to Delnabo. By the park there is a delightful relict birch wood that must have been growing here for several thousand years. The walk goes on to include some enchanting river scenery and a pleasant mix of hill and moorland. Close by the car park, a short uphill climb on Tom na Bat leads to Queen Victoria's picnic spot. From the indicator cairn there is a fine view up the glen towards distant Ben Avon.

PTARMIGAN

SPEYMOUTH - MAP & USEFUL INFORMATION

WEATHER REPORTS: 0898 500 424
TOURIST INFORMATION:
Buckie - 0542 34853, summer
Cullen - 0542 40757, summer
Lossiemouth Station Park, summer
CLYDESDALE BANK
Buckie, Cullen, Fochabers
Lossiemouth
BANK OF SCOTLAND
Buckie, Cullen, Fochabers
Lossiemouth
ROYAL BANK OF SCOTLAND
Buckie, Lossiemouth
SCOTTISH TSB
Buckie, Cullen, Lossiemouth
EARLY CLOSING:
Buckie - Wednesday
Cullen - Wednesday
Fochabers - Wednesday
Garmouth - Wednesday
Lossiemouth - Thursday

Portgordon - Wednesday
DOCTORS:
Buckie 0542 31555
Cullen 0542 40272
Fochabers 0343 820247
DENTISTS:
Buckie 0542 31163
CHEMISTS: Buckie, Cullen, Fochabers
Lossiemouth

DOTTEREL

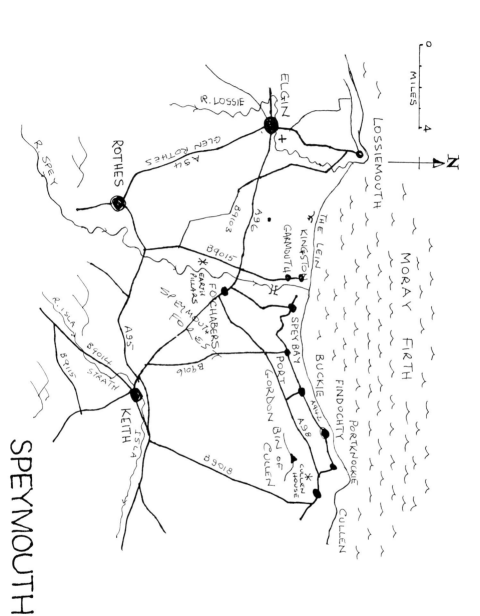

SPEYMOUTH

SPEYMOUTH - The end of the river and the road

A few miles north of Rothes, on any of the roads, there is yet another distinct and dramatic change of scenery. The surrounding hills - now noticeably smaller and softer as the river nears the sea - suddenly fall away, and there is a wonderful prospect of a broad and fertile plain with a dark blue band of ocean at the distant margin. For the river, it is nearly journey's end; for the traveller, it is the beginning of a new and different world.

The countryside is neat and clean, with well-groomed fields, tidy woods, and nicely barbered hedges. The settlement pattern perhaps owes something to the Vikings, for the arrangement of small farms with small fields on the lower slopes of the low hills has a distinctly Scandinavian flavour. The larger and richer farms, on the plain, would have come later, after the land had been drained. There is a distinct air of well-being, with comfortable farms and fat cattle; and it was the fat cattle, of course, that so attracted the caterans and freebooters of old.

People lived here long before the Norsemen came, and the district was populated by Bronze Age Beaker People, and other folk from the prehistoric past. Little is known about their daily life, but their funerary monuments remain, and they are of a type peculiar to Scotland. Recumbent stone circles occur in Perthshire, and in the north-east lowlands to the west and south of Buchan. They are found nowhere else.

They were first described more than 450 years ago, and Hector Boece (who gave the Grampians their name) had this to say in his

Historica Scotica, published in 1527:

> In the times of King Magnus ... huge stones were erected in a ring and the biggest of them was stretched out on the south side to serve for an altar, whereon were burned victims in sacrifice to the gods. In proof of the fact to this day stand these mighty stones gathered into circles - 'the old temples of the gods' they are called - and whoso sees them will surely marvel by what mechanical craft or by what bodily strength stones of such bulk have been collected to one spot.

Boece was fortunate, because he and his fellows were able to see the circles in relative entirety. All we see are the often battered remnants left by the Victorian despoilers, who dismantled and destroyed many of the finest stone circles and ring cairns. The remains are still a source of wonder and amazement, and for precisely those reasons given by Boece.

This benign and fertile countryside and the bounteous sea must have been always attractive to men. According to the Roman geographer Ptolemy it was the country of the Taezavi, and Roman artefacts have been found near Portknockie. So it is really not surprising that the oldest buildings owe something to the Normans. The major rebuilding by the Georgians swept away most of the older settlement remains, but the main commercial activities are still concerned with the soil and the sea. Populated by industrious and friendly people, the area has long been attractive to discerning holiday-makers.

On the last lap, north of Fochabers, the river writhes across the landscape like a frenzied snake, whilst the patchwork of fields and occasional scrubland have a distinctly fenland feel. There is a sense of anti-climax when the sea bursts on the scene, for with a river as mighty as the Spey it would seem reasonable to expect an estuary to scale. Perhaps it is, but it is certainly not as expected. Instead of an expansive firth, or a welter of sand banks and shoals, there is a deep and very narrow channel through a mass of shingle banks, and the river simply merges with the sea. But the stony beach of Spey Bay forms a gigantic arc in both directions, and 'spectacular' does scant justice to the scene.

To the west, eight miles of beach stretch out to the Lossie, and the hinterland is a maze of attractive little lanes. Eastwards the beach soon yields to low cliffs, the Bin of Cullen, and that litany of delightful fishing towns: Portgordon, Buckie, Portessie, Findochty, Portknockie, Cullen and Portsoy.

Roedeer

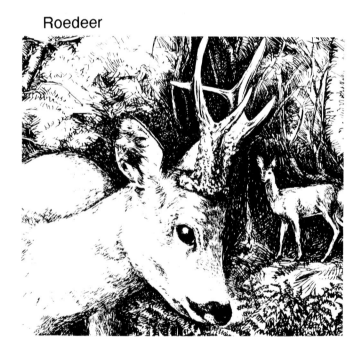

BUCKIE - Fisher town present

The landscape changes on the coast road into the town, and the cliffs ahead show that the lowland is fast running out. The Bin of Cullen, and the other diminutive and tree dappled background hills of the area, represent the last gasp of the Caledonian Orogeny. They are like the ever-decreasing ripples from a stone thrown into water, and peter out at Buckie where they meet the sea. These low hills mark the northern limit of the Grampians, and form the eastern boundary of the great lowland plain of Banff and Moray that cradles the Spey estuary, and extends westwards as far as Inverness.

With a population of around 8000, Buckie is large by local standards and is a thriving town. Tourism is of small account, and Buckie's main business is with fish. Deep-sea fishing is relatively recent here, for the Scots were late-comers on the scene. The sea around the north-east coast once teemed with fish, but right up to the 18th Cent. they were caught mainly by the Dutch - there is an old saying that '... *Amsterdam is built on Scottish herring bones.*' King Charles I established a Scottish fishery, but it took the Scots another hundred years to get down to serious business.

The heyday of fishing was the Victorian era, and the boom times led to the expansion of the town up onto the hill-top behind the harbours. The A990 coast road runs along the shore and passes by Buckpool and the Yardie - the original fishing towns. It is really worth while to spend some time wandering here, for the quaint old houses have an air of days gone by.

A little further on, the A942 is joined at Commercial Road, which runs along the harbour. This looks as every fishing harbour should and, sadly, as most do not. Between the white lighthouse and the road there is a forest of masts and a mass of fishing boats. Every type is represented here, from little inshore craft to the larger boats that fish in deep waters. At the east end of the harbour, the slipway of a ship repairer's usually has some interesting craft, which can be as varied as a modern fishing boat or an ancient steamer.

The harbour is full of craft all too often now, for set-aside doesn't just apply to farms. The boats have a limit on the days they are allowed to put to sea, and they often lie in harbour while the sea bed is stripped clean by Dutch, French and Spanish trawlers. What a farce the European 'Community' must seem to some, and how history seems to repeat itself! It is a wonder that the locals still bother to fish at all; but fishing is the ethos here, and it is undoubtedly in the blood.

Although not primarily a holiday resort, Buckie is literally a good centre for the Moray coast, since it is mid-way between Fraserburgh and Nairn. As would be expected in a town of this size, there is plenty to see and do. There no lack of cafés, restaurants, hotels and pubs., and beer drinkers should look out for the local brew from Bin Hill - the most northerly brewery in Britain. There is a swimming pool, bowling greens and tennis. There are two golf clubs: Strathlene is to the east of the town, and Buckpool, towards Portgordon, also has a squash court. Riding and pony trekking can be had at nearby Drybridge.

There is a Harbour Tour on Tuesday afternoon and Friday morning in the summer months, and it can be booked at the Tourist Information Centre in Cluny Square. The Fish Market on the quay-side is a hive of activity when fish are being landed - Friday morning is usually the best. The Buckie Maritime Museum & Peter Anson Gallery is in Cluny Place, close to Cluny Square. There is a super exhibition of the fishing industry, and the gallery houses a wonderful collection of water colours of the town and surrounding area. It is free.

CULLEN - Singing sands and a fish stew.

The old fishing villages between Buckie and Portsoy are all different, and all have their own particular attractions. At Cullen there are many interesting things to see and do, and the town is justly proud of the marvellous 'Blue Flag' beach that runs west between the headlands from the harbour - sandy beaches are none too common on this coast.

The wriggly cliffs, and the fantastic red sandstone rock formations of the bay, are in vivid contrast to the dazzling sands, and on a sunny day their combination with the bright blue sea is photogenic and quite dramatic. The sand grains are all of a size and very regular so, when stamped upon, the sands sing.

At the western entrance to the town, the road forks below the old railway viaduct and the left branch goes down to the beach, the golf course, and the little harbour, which nestles beneath the cliffs. The fishing boats have gone to Buckie, and the early 19th Cent. harbour is used now mainly by small yachts. Seatown, between the foreshore and the A98, is the oldest part of Cullen. It is the quaint, colourful and charming settlement of the original fisherfolk.

A new town was started in the 1820's, and as it expanded, Cullen could only grow one way, and that was uphill, so the steep road from the harbour through the town centre is a progression of several architectural periods and styles. They blend into an harmonious whole, and the appearance of the town is enhanced by the railway viaducts, which were imaginatively engineered - one thing the Victorians had was style. The viaducts were built because the Seafields refused to let the Great North of Scotland railway cross their land. They now frame a series of delightful prospects of the town and Cullen Bay. The arch over the main street, in the form of an old gateway, is especially attractive.

Cullen was originally sited by the Burn, and it was chartered as a Burgh by William the Lion in the 12th Cent. It later moved to Old Cullen, to the south of the present town, and the Auld Kirk is a tangible reminder of King Robert Bruce, who had much to do with its rebuilding. The church is of various dates from as far back as the Normans, but it is mainly 14th Cent. Bruce's second wife, Elizabeth de Burgh, is buried here. There is also Alexander Ogilvy's grandly extravagant tomb of 1554. South-west of the town, Cullen House, which dates from the 17th Cent., was once the home of Viscount Reidhaven - the Master of Seafield. The gardens are open to visitors on Tuesday and Friday afternoons. Further inland, the picturesque hamlet of Fordyce is built around Fordyce Castle, which is a typical tower house.

Cliff paths in both directions combine easy walking and spectacular seascapes, and an opportunity should also be found for an ascent of the Bin of Cullen, a couple of miles to the south-west of the town. On a clear day, the wonderful panorama from this lowly eminence commands wide vistas of the Firth, and looks over Ben Rinnes to the far and lofty Cairngorms.

As might be expected, there is good sea fishing, and trout anglers can try their luck in the Cullen Burn - permits from the Earl of Seafield's estate office in York Place. There are bowling greens, a nice park, and plenty of hotels, cafés, restaurants and pubs. With a delightful golf links, too, Cullen seems to have everything needed for a quiet seaside holiday.

Scotland is famous for its food, soups in particular, and the undoubted supremacy in this respect is attributed to the ancient and long connection with France. Soups and broths are relative new comers to England, and Boswell had this to say in his *Tour to the Hebrides* in 1763: *'... at dinner, Dr. Johnson ate several plates of*

Scotch broth, with barley and peas in it, and seemed very fond of the dish. I said: "You never ate it before?" - Johnson: "No, sir, but I don't care how soon I eat it again."....'

On the same tour they breakfasted at Cullen, where they were served with dried haddocks broiled, along with tea, and found them quite disgusting. Things have obviously improved since then, and Cullen Skink is a famous and most delicious fish stew that is easily made at home. Alternatively, try a tin from Baxters of Fochabers.

CULLEN SKINK

This wonderfully satisfying, yet inexpensive dish is easily prepared, and gives pleasure out of all proportion to the cost of the ingredients and the effort involved in making it.

Skin a smoked haddock, put it into a pan and cover it with boiling water. Put in a finely chopped medium sized onion, and then boil for about 10 to 15 minutes.

Take out the cooked fish, flake the flesh off the bones and put it on one side.

Put the bones back into the pan and boil them for about an hour, then strain the stock and throw away the bones.

Boil a pint of milk and add it to the stock, together with the fish flakes.

Season to taste. Bring it back to the boil and stir in sufficient mashed potato to make the stew nice and thick.

Add a lump of butter and serve the skink piping hot.

This delicious winter warmer will make two people very happy.

FINDOCHTY & PORTKNOCKIE - What's in a name?

Many visitors to Scotland will have been puzzled by the linguistic contortions apparent in such place names as Milngarvie - pronounced 'Mulguy' and Balmerino - known as 'Balmerny'. There are also strange inflections of the letter 'Z', which are possibly a throwback to the Auld Alliance and Norman French. They are seen in personal names such as Dalziel, pronounced 'Deeyell', and in the much more common name of Menzies, which all Scots, but very few others, know as 'Mingus'.

The Tourist Board likes to promote Scotland as 'The Land Of Three Languages': Gaelic, English and Scots, and there are some interesting local examples of the latter. The medieval name for the land between Buckie and the Spey was the Burgh of Enzie, pronounced 'Ingy'' (is the Ross-shire clan Mackenzie called 'Mackingy'?) 'Skink' is a lovely old Scots name for a stew, and it is the one thing most outsiders associate with Cullen. As for Findochty, the fact that the locals call the town 'Fineckty' should, by now, occasion no surprise.

Findochty and Portknockie have several things in common with the other little towns along this coast: they have many 18th Cent. buildings, they are old fishing ports, and they have a timeless and relaxing air. Findochty harbour is extremely picturesque, but nowadays it holds mainly small inshore craft, and all the big working boats have gone to Buckie.

The quaint little pub by the Victorian harbour here is exactly what it seems, and it looks out onto a colourful scene. The old houses on the far side of the harbour are built end-on to the sea as protection from the winter weather. On the rise behind the harbour the newer houses stand four square in their stolid Victorian respectability, and the Church of Scotland is in a most unlikely spot, on a little knoll beside the sea.

Although the climate is quite mild, it can still blow a bit in winter, and many of the houses are rendered and painted to keep out the wet. The paint isn't ordinary colour wash, it is oil colour, which gives scope for the use of many different hues. It is the colour that is long remembered, and at first sight these little ports seem to have more in common with the Mediterranean than the North Sea.

Built atop a green and pleasant headland, nearby Portknockie overlooks the broad expanses of the Moray Firth. It dates back to the 17th Cent., and was founded by fishermen displaced from Old Cullen. Unlike its neighbours, it is a cliff-top village, with a steep track down to the old harbour, which is accessible at any state of the tide.

Nowadays the usual customers seem to be small sailing boats, and the harbour looks very like a continental marina. On a typical summer's day the sight of the yachts, the intense blue of the sea and sky, the red rocks and white sand, all add to the distinctly Mediterranean air.

Much of Portknockie and Findochty are conservation areas, and there is obviously a great deal of local pride in the towns.

They are singularly attractive places, quite different from each other in appearance, but very similar in size and the warmth of the welcome extended to visitors.

Both towns have sites for touring caravans. There is bowling and tennis, and plenty of rock pools to splash about in. Golfers have a choice of Buckie Strathlene, which runs to Findochty, or Cullen's excellent links immediately to the east of Portknockie.

FOCHABERS - Cockpit of the north

In the 18th Cent., Speyside was dominated by two great land-owning families: the Gordons and the Grants. The Duke of Gordon - the 'Cock of the North' - had a vast estate that extended from the seaside of the Moray Firth right across the country, over the Monadhliaths, and deep into Lochaber. The Gordons had many substantial residences, but the ducal seat was Gordon Castle at Fochabers, in the Laich of Moray.

The original six-storey tower house was built at the end of the 15th Cent. on an earlier foundation. About three hundred years and many additions later, the 4th Duke decided that it was just a bit out of date. He therefore remodelled and extended it, so that he could have a more comfortable abode. In the process he decided that the little village just outside the castle walls would have to go, since he considered that it would rather spoil the prospect from his new home. His opinion seems to have been endorsed by no less an authority than James Boswell.

On his way to the Hebrides in 1763, Dr. Samuel Johnson passed by here in the company of his biographer. Boswell considered Gordon Castle to be princely looking, but remarked that Fochabers was a poor place, with many of the houses ruinous. This was, of course, an era of rebuilding, and it is reasonable to suppose that some Government money was involved, but subsidised or not, it didn't matter, for Fochabers was not eradicated: it was moved.

The result of all this new construction was the pleasant little town that exists today. A typical planned town of the Georgian era, with the streets laid out in a rectangular grid, the building was done in the attractive warm-toned local stone. This is an elegant place with a wealth of interesting architecture, particularly around The Square. Most of the town centre is conserved, and the only discordant note is the busy A96 trunk road that runs along the High Street and bisects the town.

Before Fochabers was moved, travellers had to use a ferry for the river crossing. A new bridge was built in 1804, on the outskirts of the town, but it stood for only a quarter of a century, and was badly damaged by the mighty floods of 1829. It was patched up, but the repairs were evidently inadequate, and in 1854 it was replaced by the elegant bridge in use today.

The new town was planned by a man called Baxter, and at the mention of this name all gourmets' heads should bow in silent tribute. Baxters of Speyside are world-renowned as purveyors of superb and sometimes exotic foods. The brainchild of one of the gardeners at Gordon Castle, the business started life in the 19th Cent. as a little shop on Spey Street. The shop was soon outgrown, and the firm's headquarters and visitor centre are now on the outskirts of the town near Mosstodloch.

A visit to Baxters must not be missed by anyone on holiday within reasonable distance of Fochabers. Allow plenty of time, for a visit can easily occupy half a day: there is so much to see and do. After an audio-visual show, a factory tour illustrates how the high quality produce of the local fisheries and countryside is selected, prepared and packed. The firm does not live entirely in the past, and the Experimental Kitchen is constantly devising new products to enhance the existing range.

The Old Shop Museum, which is a faithful reproduction of the original Spey Street store, provides a fascinating glimpse of times gone by, and a feast of nostalgia for older visitors. The 'Mrs. Baxter's Kitchen' brand in The Victorian Kitchen is a special range of foods that cannot be bought elsewhere. Also on sale are unusual gift items and kitchen utensils, and there are yet more products in the

George Baxter cellar. There is much more to see and do, inside and out, and when aching feet call a halt there is a café/restaurant with good food.

Back in Fochabers, Pringle Church on High Street is the unlikely setting for the superb museum created by Gordon Christie. This is a private museum, and a small payment secures admission to a unique collection of horse-drawn vehicles, and to a folk museum which nicely illustrates the development of the town, and the changing way of life in Fochabers down the years. It perfectly complements the Highland Folk Museum, far upstream in Kingussie.

Alexander Milne left the town and went to America, following a disagreement with his employer, the 5th Duke. The cause of the dispute was his long hair, but he was certainly not a layabout. He went to New Orleans, and made a substantial fortune as a builder - most of the harbour is his work. Returning to his native town, he bequeathed $100,000 for the establishment of a free school, and the imposing Victorian structure of Milne's High School, on High Street, was the happy result.

When Jane Maxwell died in 1812 the Duke of Gordon married Jean Christie, and the name still seems to dominate the town. Christies have an excellent garden centre at the junction of the Buckie and Aberdeen roads, with many things of interest to non-gardeners. There is a tea room.

There is plenty of easy walking in the vicinity, both on the Speyside way, which passes by the town, and in the vast woodlands of Speymouth Forest. Once Gordon property, this great woodland is now the province of Forestry Enterprise - the Forestry Commission in disguise. The 'Earth Pillars' of Aultdearg are near to the forest picnic area, on the minor road to Ordquiesh, about a mile south of the town. Hardly a walk but not to be missed, these are fantastic columns of weathered Old Red sandstone conglomerate, that tower above the Spey.

A swimming pool - unusual in the area - can be enjoyed at

Burnside Caravan Park, on the Keith road, and there is tennis, bowling and putting in the town.

Kestrel

COCKS OF THE NORTH - The Gordon Dynasty.

Of Norman origin, the Gordons were always a force to be reckoned with, and were constantly at odds with their powerful Strathspey rivals, the Grants, the Macintoshes and the Macphersons. The antipathy had ancient roots that dated back over 900 years, for the Comyns and the Gordons were Norman overlords who came over with William the Conqueror, and their presence was, naturally, resented by the native Highland Celts. The Comyns land was forfeit to the Crown in Robert Bruce's reign, and in the 15th Cent. James II gave Badenoch to the Earl of Huntly, who was a Gordon. So the Gordon dominance in Strathspey lasted for some 500 years.

By the 16th Cent. they were thought to be too powerful, and were causing all sorts of trouble for the Crown. In 1562 Queen Mary set out for Speyside to remind John Gordon, the 4th Earl, just who was in charge. Summoned to Aberdeen, the Earl ignored the royal command, so Mary and her army marched on to Inverness. Here, in an act of great bravery and great stupidity, the Earl's younger brother, the castle Governor, refused to admit the Queen. For his temerity and treason Mary hanged him from the castle battlements. Later on, the Earl was brought to heel on Deeside.

After this rebuff, the Gordons kept their heads down for some time and quietly prospered. At Fochabers, the original 16th Cent. tower house of the Gordons was built in the centre of the Bog of Gight, and could be entered only via a narrow causeway and drawbridge. The resident Gordons were referred to as the Guidmen of the Bog. Some two hundred years later the morass had been drained, and a great castle stood in more than a thousand acres of glorious parkland.

The 4th Duke had married Lady Jane Maxwell, but they were an oddly assorted couple and tended to go their own ways. The Duke was a great improver, and built many of the Georgian new towns in Strathspey. The Duchess spent much of her time at Kinrara, a little way upstream from Aviemore, and she also graced the London season, where she was a great favourite of George III. It is supposed that Pitt was often cajoled into finding good posts for her favourites from Badenoch and Strathspey.

As a result of a wager with the Prince Regent, she became one of the most famous and successful recruiters for the army during the Napoleonic wars. She used to travel round Strathspey with a piper, and dance with any likely recruits. They were rewarded with a guinea and a kiss from the Duchess. In this manner she is reputed to have raised, practically single handed, the entire 92nd Regiment - The Gordon Highlanders.

By this time, whatever ill feeling had existed between the Gordons and the Rothiemurchus Grants was long dead, and Elizabeth Grant wrote of the happy times spent at Kinrara in the company of the much older Duchess. There was general and genuine mourning when Jane Maxwell died in 1812, and Mrs. Allarsdyce's elegy expressed the popular feeling:

> ".... When was called forth our youth to arms,
> Her eye inspired each martial spirit;
> Her mind, too, felt the Muse's charms,
> And gave the meed to modest merit.
> But now, farewell, fair northern star,
> Thy beams no more shall Courts enlighten,
> No more lead youth, our youth, to war,
> No more the rural pastures brighten...."

The direct line of Gordons expired with the death, in 1836, of

George, the 5th Duke, whose commemorative column towers above the summit of Tor Alvie, near Kincraig. When the 5th Duke died the estate passed to the Duke of Richmond and Lennox, but the style was changed to Richmond and Gordon in 1876 to maintain the Gordon name. Following the death of a Duke of Richmond and Gordon in 1935, the majority of the estate became Crown lands, and Gordon Castle was largely demolished some twenty years later. Thus virtually ended a family history that could fill several books.

GARMOUTH & KINGSTON - The end of the river and the road.

A quiet country road, the B9105, that turns north from the A96 at Mosstodloch, leads into a stretch of quite delightful countryside. In spring the road is a verdant ribbon, brightly bordered by green and saffron hedgerows of gorse and broom. But even the broom seems drab in comparison with the brash and vivid yellow of the oilseed rape, growing in the bordering fields. A little stand of Scots pine, on the right near Garmouth, is a mute reminder of the forests that have now been left behind. The road ends nearby, on the very edge of the ocean where the Spey ends its long journey to the sea.

This location at the mouth of the Spey would have been a strategically important place, and people lived here in prehistoric times. A 12th Cent. gift of land to a Norman noble is recorded, and this Norman was a forbear of the local Innes family. Another local family, the Duffs, gained the Earldom of Fife. Incidentally, it was the 2nd Earl who first rented, and then sold, Balmoral to Queen Victoria.

Garmouth was, for long, the chief port for the Laich of Moray, and so it was at Garmouth that Charles II landed in 1650. He signed the Solemn League and Covenant, designed to impose universal Presbytarianism, in a house in the town. Charles was acknowledged in Scotland as the 'Covenanted King', which rather upset Cromwell, and the ensuing battles of Dunbar and Worcester sent Charles on his travels once more. Ten years later the Restoration brought Charles back again.

Around the nucleus of a few isolated houses, Kingston was built in 1784 by two Yorkshiremen, who had bought timber in the

Gordon forests in Glenmore, many miles away upstream. The Gordon timber, along with that from the nearby Grant woodlands of Rothiemurchus, was floated down to Garmouth as huge rafts. The village was established to support the shipyard they shrewdly started here, and in a fit of nostalgia they named it Kingston, as a reminder of their native Humber town. Typical of many coastal villages, Kingston, and its elder sister Garmouth, are built in a snug huddle with a maze of narrow streets. In Garmouth it is easy to imagine that the sea is far away.

However unlikely it may seem today, this was once an important ship-building centre, and many shipyards lined the river bank and shoreline. For some thirty years from around the end of the 18th Cent., the yards produced merchant ships and men-o-war. And then, almost as quickly as it had blossomed, the industry declined at the end of the Napoleonic war and the Yorkshiremen went home. A lone local shipwright struggled on, but the local firm eventually subsided, a victim of the growth of Clydeside and of iron ships.

As a really mortal blow, the great floods of 1829 altered the river's course again, and the change was so drastic that it left the villages stranded high and dry. So ended Garmouth's role as a port, and seabirds now peck amongst the marshland where sailing ships used to lie, loading and discharging their cargoes.

The late Victorian era saw a mushrooming of the railways, and the Great North of Scotland line from Aberdeen to Inverness crossed the Spey at Garmouth. The huge viaduct, some 300 yards long, has a series of lattice girders, and a great arch as the central span. When the bridge was built in 1886 the arch spanned the river, but not for long, and two years later, in one of its characteristic violent swings, the Spey changed course, and the arch now spans dry land. So much for the grand designs of man!

Now the railway, too, has gone, but the viaduct remains and it provides a handy footway across the Spey. It joins the Speyside Way on the east bank of the river, and it makes a pleasant walking route to Tugnet Ice House, or to Fochabers. Tugnet is the best place to go to see the river flow into the sea, and having come this far, that is what every visitor should do.

For some, the main attraction of Kingston is the Lein, a remarkable reserve administered by the Scottish Wildlife Trust. It is an enormous area of shingle bank created progressively since the last ice age, partly by changing sea levels and partly by long-shore drift and storms. Nearly as big as Chesil Bank, the undulating ridges and hollows of the Lein contain many rare and unusual plants in the many different habitats. Birdwatchers have a bonus here because sea ducks, cormorants, waders and many other birds are attracted to the estuary and the beach. Offshore there are seals and the Moray dolphins.

This expansive lowland seems a world away from the mountains, and the long stony beaches have much in common with the shingle and the high skies of Suffolk. This is very much an area where nature reigns, and where the hustle and bustle of the work-a-day world seem very remote. It is easy here to be quite alone, with just thoughts, and the sounds of the wind and sea for company.

A network of very quiet and very minor roads stretches away to the west, towards Lossiemouth and Elgin. By Lockhill, about three miles from Garmouth, Innes House has delightful gardens that are open to the public on summer weekdays. The house itself is not open to visitors. Near to the crossroads, a little way to the south, the remains of a recumbent stone circle of some 40 yards diameter is a reminder of the area's early history. South again, there was another, smaller, circle near to Bogton Mill. Also near Lhanbryde, picturesque Coxton Tower stands by B9103. A 17th Cent. tower house, harled to exclude the weather, it has an iron yett, and outside steps have been built where a ladder once served for access.

There is boat fishing for trout at Loch na Bo (the Loch of the cattle) by the B9103 at Lhanbryde. At Kingston there is sea fishing from the beach, but as this is a Crown fishery a permit is required - see the Fishing chapter.

GARMOUTH VIADUCT - SPEY BAY

PORTGORDON - Fisher town past

From Spey Bay a little road starts from near the Garmouth rail-bed track, and follows the coast via Nether Dallochy to Portgordon. On the way it passes interesting reminders of World War II. There is a remnant airfield where the old control towers are spotty concrete, and the glassless window openings make stark black patches, in marked contrast to the vivid orange lichen on the walls. There are old hangars in red painted corrugated iron, now used agriculturally, and a concrete runway of incredible length - now breaking up, and dotted with green and weedy patches. A gliding club is in occupation, so the old airfield is useful even now.

Another brainchild of the 4th Duke of Gordon, and built in 1797, Portgordon looks exactly what it is: a quiet and sleepy little seaside village that time abandoned many years ago. It wasn't always so, and for a period after World War I it outdid Arbroath and Auchmithie as a line fishery, and was also a busy herring port. Modern boats are too big for the Victorian harbour, and it is now left with a few pleasure craft and many dreams.

The main road is joined beyond the harbour, and the road to the right leads through the Braes of Enzie straight to Keith. This is a quick and direct way into the hills, which now seem very far away. Straight on from the junction, the road to Buckie runs by the old railway embankment, which shelters Buckpool golf course on the right. At Gollachy, midway between the village and the town, an old ice-house stands on seaside turf between the roadway and the shore. Much smaller than its companion at Tugnet, it is a listed building, and has been recently restored.

SPEY BAY & TUGNET - Salmon, shingle & sea breezes

It is hard to imagine what life would be like without all the familiar trappings and equipment of the day. Even older generations tend to forget that polythene bags were still uncommon only forty years ago, as were fridges and freezers. In the winter there were salted beans, Kilner jars of fruit, and lots of jam and pickles. Many foodstuffs, including meat and fish, were seasonal.

Preservation and storage were a problem in the past, and it was difficult to keep things fresh until they arrived at their destinations. The commercial salmon fisheries on the Spey had a particularly serious dilemma, being far from their best markets. Over the centuries various forms of preservation, such as salting and pickling, were tried without success, but about 150 years ago it was discovered that ice would do the job. The subsequent coming of the railways, and then better roads, solved the problem, and ice packing is still in use today.

The early 19th Cent. ice-house of Tugnet is the largest in Scotland, and is a superb example of its kind. Built deep down in the shingle banks, which provide insulation and maintain an even temperature, the turf-covered roof arches are about all that can be seen above ground. The small square openings that face the sea were used for loading ice, and the entrance is through a tunnel, excavated at the rear. Nowadays the ice-house is an exhibition complex which tells the story of the salmon fishing industry, and explains and illustrates the varied wildlife of the Spey estuary. It is open every day from June to September.

The fishery here was once the Duke of Gordon's preserve, and it passed to the Crown some sixty years ago. It is still operating on a small scale from the Fishery Station building nearby. This, again, is typical of its kind, with fish packing at ground level, and net storage lofts beneath the eaves.

The Spey estuary is not, perhaps, what might be expected: there is no mighty firth as with the Tay, or great port like Aberdeen; instead, the brown stream runs strongly, far into the ocean, and incoming tides hardly affect the flow. So the river simply fizzles out with scarcely a ripple, as the immensely deep but narrow channel meets the sea. A surprise, maybe, but not a disappointment; and standing on the shingle it is possible to imagine a great estuary that extended from Lossiemouth to Buckie as the ice-age ended. Here, the rest of the world seems far away, and there is a great sense of loneliness and isolation that is not at all unpleasant.

Now the water has receded and the land has risen, and the vast acres of shingle banks lie in serried ranks and rows. Inland, towards the viaduct at Garmouth, there is a welter of stony hummocks, old channels, marsh and scrubland through which the river twists and turns. It is a fossil river system, and the history of past channel changes is quite clear. It was to give a degree of permanence to the river mouth that the present deep channel was dredged some years ago. Prior to that the shifts were very frequent.

There is not a lot to Spey Bay, just a few - mainly single storey - houses, a caravan site, the golf links and the hotel. It is a place for golfers, bird watchers, lovers of peace and solitude, and sea views. This is a bracing sort of place with a healthy tang of salt on the wind. But the wind is not the perishing north-easter one might reasonably expect, and on the Moray Firth a stiff summer breeze often has more balm than bite.

The ocean bird life is rich and varied, and there are many waders, and wildfowl. An osprey is the subject of the David Annand sculpture at the ice-house and, as the Scottish osprey population is now quite large, there is always a possibility in summer that one of these birds will be seen fishing the estuary.

TUGNET-ICE HOUSES & SHINGLE BANKS

LAICH OF MORAY - MAP & USEFUL INFORMATION

TOURIST INFORMATION:
Elgin - 0343 542666
Forres - 0309 72938, summer
Lossiemouth Station Park, summer
Nairn - 0667 52753, summer
CLYDESDALE BANK
Elgin, Forres, Lossiemouth, Nairn
BANK OF SCOTLAND
Elgin, Forres, Lossiemouth, Nairn
ROYAL BANK OF SCOTLAND
Elgin, Forres, Lossiemouth, Nairn
SCOTTISH TSB
Elgin, Forres, Lossiemouth, Nairn
WEATHER REPORTS: 0898 500 424
EARLY CLOSING:
Elgin - Wednesday, MD - Frid.
Forres - Wednesday, MD - Tues.
Lossiemouth - Thursday
Nairn - Wednesday, MD - Thurs.
DOCTORS:
Elgin - 0343 542225

Forres - 0309 72221
DENTISTS:
Elgin - 0343 542697
Forres - 0309 72631
CHEMISTS
  Elgin, Forres, Lossiemouth
  Nairn

Peregrine

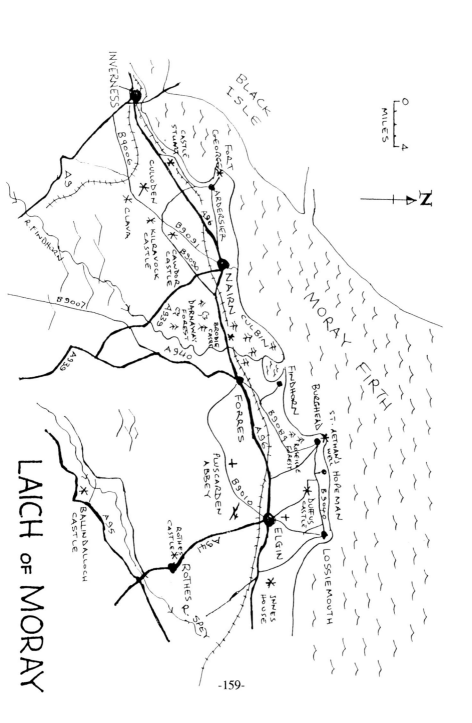

LAICH OF MORAY

BLACK ISLE

INVERNESS

MORAY FIRTH

NAIRN

FORRES

ELGIN

LOSSIEMOUTH

MILES 0 4

N

-159-

THE LAICH OF MORAY - The Garden of Scotland

Between the rivers Nairn and Lossie the great swathe of fertile fields and lush woodland, that extends from the shore to the low hills in the south, has for long been known as the Laich, Laidh or Laigh of Moray. An area of rich farmland, and with a dry and gentle climate, the district also has been called - somewhat fancifully - the Scottish Riviera and, with much more justification, the Garden of Scotland.

The Laich (pronounced 'Lie') is a broad plain that starts around sea level, and rises to about 500 feet where it quietly changes, first to pasture, and then to grouse moor. As is usually the case, the physical characteristics of the district can be attributed to a combination of geology and location.

The base is probably of ancient rocks on which a Mesozoic layer was first laid down and then removed again. The ancient base is exposed here and there as Old Red sandstone (which actually varies in colour from dark red to buff), but the majority of the area is covered by a deep layer of glacial drift. It is the drift, a complex layer deposited from the melting ice, that forms the basis of the rich and fertile soils.

This low-lying littoral plain is bounded inland by high mountains, and these protect the Laich from all the bad weather that the Atlantic throws at it from the north, west and south. It is true that it is exposed to the east, and this is why the Moray coast rarely resembles the Riviera, for the winds here are often strong, and they can be very cold.

Wild Cats.
A.R.Thomas.

That said, it is a place where snow does not lie, where there is very little frost, and where the rainfall is only about 24 inches per year - which makes it one of the drier parts of Britain. It is also the reason why the RAF has two important bases here - for the weather permits flying on every day of the year.

The merits of the area have been recognised for ages, and Daniel Defoe had this to say in 1724: '..*Murray (Moray) is, indeed a pleasant country, the soil fruitful, watered with fine rivers, and full of good towns, but especially of gentlemen's seats, more and more remarkable than could, indeed, be expected by a stranger in so remote part of the country.*' He went on to remark on the high quality and variety of the crops, and the early harvest, very often as early as in some parts of Kent.

The Laich of Moray has a long and varied history, and there is a great deal of local pride in the Moray heritage. There are many remains of occupation by prehistoric people, there are Iron Age forts and impressive remnants of the great monastic age, there are intriguing ruins, and old fishing ports and seaside villages galore. There are fabulous old castles, and stately homes, and, in the towns, a wealth of Georgian architecture and superb museums.

It should be evident, then, why people have lived here happily all through the ages, and the qualities that make it such a good place in which to live also make Moray a great place for a holiday. The inland towns of Elgin and Forres, although not tourist towns as such, contain much of interest, and they make good bases for touring much of Speyside. The coastal towns are deservedly well known, and have long catered for discerning holiday makers of all ages.

It is not all seaside and stately homes, and there is a varied countryside that includes large areas of peaceful woodland, and some of Britain's finest river scenery. There are many happy places in the Laich of Moray, and far more things to see and do than can be covered in one brief holiday. One thing is fairly certain: the first visit will not be the last; and visitors have a tendency to come back often.

BURGHEAD - Ancient mysteries and a memorable beach

The protracted ending of the last ice age was marked by several stages, the traces of which are still quite evident today. The melting ice released vast quantities of mineral debris that formed the basis of the present soils, and which is known to geologists as drift. Relieved of the tremendous mass of ice, the land rose slowly from the sea, and succesive old beach platforms mark the various stages of the thaw.

At the beginning of the Iron Age a large tract of land between Burghead and Lossiemouth, to the north of Elgin, was virtually a small offshore island. It was connected to the mainland only by a shingle spit at the western end, and a narrow, shallow brackish lagoon ran along the coast between Roseisle and the Lossie. It would have been an easily defended redoubt in troubled times and, not surprisingly, it has yielded many archaeological remains.

In common with the other coastal settlements, modern Burghead owes its existence to the sea. This pleasant little fishing village is built on the promonotory at the eastern end of Burghead Bay, and the quiet little 19th Cent. harbour, nestling on the S. side of the headland, shelters its many fishing boats from virtually any sort of blow.

The little museum has, amongst many other interesting things, casts of the Burghead Pictish stones, the originals of which now repose in London in the British Museum. Why does all that is best in Britain have to be removed from its locality and spirited away to London or Edinburgh: couldn't they have the replicas?

Burghead has a romantic past, and the headland is guarded by the vitrified stone ramparts of a Pictish fort. Much was destroyed when the 19th Cent. harbour was built, but within its bounds there is another treasure whose purpose is still far from clear. St. Aethan's Well, which is cut deep down into the rock, was discovered in 1809 by workmen prospecting for a new water supply. Many Roman artefacts were dug up in the process and, as Roman remains had been found at many places on the south side of the Firth, the well was presumed to be a Roman bath (bergh, burgh or burg in an English place name usually indicates a Roman site).

Elizabeth Grant visited the well in the year of its discovery, and some forty years later she had this to say about that exciting day:

> '....on going lower the workmen came upon a bath, a spring enclosed by cut stone walls, a mosaic pavement surrounding the bath, steps descending to it, and paintings upon the walls....We had all of us great pleasure in going to see these curious remains of past ages thus suddenly brought to light....I remember regretting that the walls were in many parts defaced.'

An Edwardian roof has replaced the original vault, and current opinion identifies the spring as an early Christian baptistry, or perhaps a Celtic Iron Age bath, contemporary with the fort.

Other pagan echoes still exist in Burghead, and there is a ritual burning of a Clavie - a tar barrel - on January 11th, the eve of old Yuletide. The barrel is fired on Dorrie Hill, a little mound on the promontory, and is then carried round the town to 'ward-off evil spirits.' The remains are deposited at the Clavie Stone. Although it is thought to be a pre-Christian ritual, this may be a survival from the Norsemens' days. There is more than a passing resemblance to Lerwick's pagan fire festival of 'Up Helly Aa', and Viking Torffness may well have been located here.

South of the village, the Corsican pines of the extensive Roseisle Forest provide both shelter and a backdrop to the stupendous and lonely sands of Burghead Bay. This expanse of glorious beach stretches in a vast unbroken arc to Findhorn, some eight miles to the west. On the B9089, some five miles south of the village, a track leads through the forest for about a mile to a car park and picnic area. This is the place to come to for solitude and seaside on a warm summer's day.

Watchers by the shore

ELGIN - An abundance of antiquity and elegance

In an attractive location on the south bank of the Lossie, Elgin is the capital of Moray - the 'Riviera and garden of the North'. It is busy and prosperous, yet is also a quiet, and most pleasant and elegant little place. It was not always so, and it has had its ups and downs. It was once a cathedral city, as local road signs emphasise as they point to the 'City Centre'.

The remains of the cathedral, which dates from the 14th Cent., never fail to impress, and it was built on an even earlier foundation. In 1390 the old cathedral, and much of Elgin and the nearby town of Forres, were burnt down by the notorious outlawed 'Wolf of Badenoch', a bastard son of Robert II. He had been excommunicated by the Bishop and, riding out with his forces from his stronghold in the island castle of Lochindorb, this was his violent riposte. Incidentally, the 'Wolf' died soon afterwards, and he had evidently made his peace with the bishop because he was buried in Dunkeld cathedral. You can see his tomb there today, with his effigy on top, resting in Christian composure - an image far removed from the wild reality.

Elgin cathedral was rebuilt, but in 1506 the steeple fell down, and it, too, had to be rebuilt. The building escaped the destructive excesses of the Reformation, but the roof was stripped of lead in 1568 in an abortive attempt to raise money to pay the local soldiery. The attempt failed because the ship carrying the lead to Holland foundered in a storm. After this local example of Divine retribution the building suffered from various acts of 17th Cent. official

ELGIN - HIGH STREET

vandalism that effectively ruined the interior. In 1711 the steeple fell down again. That was the end of the attempts to rebuild, and the 'Lanthorn of the North' rapidly fell into a state of more or less complete disrepair.

Despite its history of desecration and neglect, the cathedral is a most spectacular and beautiful ruin. Much of interest remains, and the Chapter house and west front are particularly noteworthy. So, too, are the Panns Port, or East Gate, and the remains of the 15th Cent. Bishop's Palace. There are many interesting memorials, including a 6th Cent. Pictish stone. Amongst many quaint inscriptions on tombstones, that of John Geddes and his wife, dated 1687, is quite well known and offers much food for thought:

> *This world is a citie full of streets &*
> *Death is the mercat that all men meets.*
> *If life were a thing that monie could buy*
> *The poor could not live & the rich would not die.*

The present town centre still closely follows the medieval street pattern, and is an attractive composite of 18th and 19th Cent. houses, shops and inns built in the warm-toned local stone. Here and there, a coat of colour-wash adds variety, and it should come as no surprise to learn that much of the material used for domestic building in the 18th Cent. town was salvaged from the wreck of the cathedral.

There are some older buildings dotted about and, like many Scottish towns, Elgin has a long, wide High Street. Here, this quite magnificent thoroughfare is dominated by the classical facade of St. Giles' Kirk, and is further enhanced by the many fine buildings on either hand. A 17th Cent. Little Cross at the east end of the street contrasts with a much restored Muckle (big) Cross at what was the old market place. At the far west end of the street, the Duke of Gordon's column arises from the rubble of the 13th Cent. castle on Lady hill.

Braco's Banking, down the street from the Tourist Information Centre and near to the Little Cross, is a fine (albeit slightly modified) example of an 17th Cent. arcaded 'piazza' house. There are many interesting side streets, and old arcades, alley ways and wynds. Academy Street, in particular, has many charming examples of the sort of architecture that must help to make this such a pleasant place in which to live.

Despite its turbulent past, Elgin has an almost tangible air of peace and tranquillity. It is a light and airy place with many green and open spaces, and many elegant and attractive shops. The residents are friendly folk who seem to be well aware of their good fortune in living here whilst we are merely visitors. It is a good place in which to shop, to eat and to drink, or simply idly to pass the time of day. The small museum is a model of its kind.

Although not normally thought of as a tourist town, Elgin has all the amenities and facilities of a large holiday resort. There are tennis courts, bowling greens, a swimming pool, and fishing in the Lossie and local lochs, including that at Millbuie Park, at the entrance to Glen Rothes, and there is also some excellent walking country here. The fine parkland golf course is by the Birnie road, at the southern edge of the town.

In addition to the town museum in High street, the Moray Motor Museum, just across the river on the road to Lossiemouth, has a collection calculated to turn the average motoring enthusiast green with envy.

Between Elgin and Forres the roadside woodlands alternate with stretches of open countryside. This is indeed the 'Garden of the North', and there are long views across vast expanses of rich chocolate coloured soil and lush crops. The woodlands are very varied, too, and alongside the ubiquitous conifers there are birch, beech, sycamore and cherry.

Between the towns, on a well signposted minor road off B9010, Pluscarden Abbey is a unique monastic house that should be on everybody's visiting list. The original priory, dating back to 1230, fell into disuse at the Reformation. About forty years ago its lay owner gave it to the Benedictines from Prinknash Abbey, and they started a restoration that is still going on. It is now open every day, and there is much to admire and enjoy.

FORRES - Macbeth, the America's Cup & the mystery of the sands

William Shakespeare made Forres famous, and the town's name is known throughout the world. As everyone should be aware from *The Tragedy of Macbeth*, Banquo and Macbeth were on their way to Duncan's castle when they encountered the three witches on Hardmuir's blasted heath, and Banquo uttered the immortal words: *"How far is't called to Forres?"* What most Shakespeare buffs fail to realise is that Duncan and Macbeth were real people, and that Duncan did, in fact, have a castle somewhere in the vicinity. Macbeth's castle was at Inverness.

Malcolm II was the first monarch to be recognised as King of the Scots, and Duncan succeeded him in 1034. Duncan was an Atholl, at odds with the Morays, and when Macbeth killed him in 1040, not far from Duffus, the Morays regained the throne. That was how it was done in those far-off days, and Macbeth, contrary to the Shakespearean slander, was a pretty good king who reigned for seventeen years.

Forres has existed in some form or other for a very long time, and it may have been the *Pinnata Castra* on Ptolemy's map of 200 AD. However, Forres then is not Forres now, for the original settlement, which was closer to the sea, was engulfed by the Culbin Sands. The present town has a medieval street pattern, but the oldest existing buildings date back only to the 18th Cent. There are many historic associations, and there was once a castle on the little hill at the west end of High Street. It is reasonable to assume that the original, which would have been built of wood, was the seat of the early Scottish kings.

Sueno's Stone is the most remarkable monolith in Scotland. Surrounded by iron railings, it stands by the Findhorn road on the outskirts of the town. About 20 feet high, it is intricately carved with martial scenes in a style similar to the Saxon cross at Gosforth. Dating from around 1000 AD, it may have commemorated the final victory over the Norsemen, and it could be contemporary with Duncan and Macbeth - a romantic possibility.

In Victoria Road, on the edge of Grant Park, and not far from Sueno's Stone, something that looks like a cracked boulder is a memorial of a rather different kind. It is said to mark the place where some poor wretch met her end. A plaque carries the following inscription:

> From Cluny Hill witches were rolled in stout barrels
> through which spikes were driven. Where the barrels
> stopped they were burned with their mangled contents.
> This stone marks the site of one such spot.

On the other side of the railings, in Grant Park, various paths lead through the woods to the top of the hill and the elegant octagonal tower of the Nelson Memorial. It is a superb viewpoint, and the little exhibition inside can be seen on weekday afternoons in the summer. The park is a delightful place, and the summer flower displays are gloriously colourful.

The Falconer Museum is located with the Tourist Information Centre near to the Tolbooth in the town centre. It has a variety of permanent displays relating to Forres and the surrounding area, and is open all year. There are all the amenities of a big town, including swimming, bowling and tennis. There is loch and river fishing, riding, pony trekking, and golf.

Further afield, Brodie Castle, three miles down the road to Inverness, is now owned by the National Trust for Scotland. The original building, which dated from the 12th Cent., was destroyed in 1645, and the present magnificent castle was built between the 17th and 19th Cents. The interior has fine furnishings and paintings, but the greatest interest lies, perhaps, in the surrounding parkland and gardens. The house is open from Monday to Saturday during the summer months, and the gardens are open all the year round.

Charles St. John, a celebrated naturalist and hunter, lived in nearby Elgin. Arguably a far more entertaining author than Gilbert White, he wrote a marvellous book: *Wild Sports in the Highlands*. First published in 1845, it still makes excellent and entertaining reading. He had this to say: *'I do not know a stream that more completely realises all one's ideas of the beauty of Highland scenery than the Findhorn.....from source to mouth this river is full of beauty and interest'*.

Findhorn Bay is about six miles north of Forres on B9091, and this remarkable lagoon-like river estuary is a water-sporting Paradise. Findhorn village is a tiny little place across the water from the Culbin forest. It gained brief fame and notoriety in 1991 when the Royal Findhorn Yacht Club had the temerity to challenge for the America's Cup. Unfortunately there was insufficient sponsorship money forthcoming, and Findhorn relapsed into its normal state of peace and serenity.

Once an important port, salmon fishery and ship building centre, it is now dedicated to sailing, water skiing and canoeing. There are picnic sites and many sheltered nooks amongst the dunes. The magnificent sands of Burghead Bay stretch away to the east, and they are fine for sea bathing. DO NOT BATHE IN FINDHORN BAY.

Some of the finest river scenery in Britain can be enjoyed quite close to Forres. About four miles south, on A940, there is a car park by the Mains of Sluie. A sign-posted walk leads through some delightful mature woodland to a remarkable river gorge. The water has worn away the sandstone here, and the 200 foot deep chasm is truly breathtaking. About a mile further south, another car park is conveniently placed for the way-marked route to the so-called

Randolph's Leap. At this fantastic spot the river thunders through a deep abyss that is only eight feet wide.

To the west of Findhorn Bay and north of the A96 lies a stretch of woodland with a remarkable history. In the 17th Cent. the Barony of Culbin was an area of farmland, as rich as any in the Laich of Moray. It was edged with great sandhills along the coast, not unlike those to the east of Lossiemouth. The sandhills were naturally stabilised by the marram grass, common in any area of dunes. Unfortunately for Culbin, the local peasants found that marram grass made an ideal thatch. They stripped out the grass in vast quantities, and the dunes were gradually denuded.

Towards the end of 1694 a period of severe north-westerly gales started to move the sand inland, and once started there was no stopping it. According to local legend the disaster happened overnight, but experience elsewhere suggests a gradual encroachment. What is not in question is that the whole of Culbin, an area of some twenty square miles, was engulfed in sand and turned from farmland into desert. Even the Findhorn estuary was blocked, and the river, which once flowed into the Firth by Buckie Loch, had to cut itself a new course to the east.

Not so long ago this was an area of great and mobile dunes, and it looked quite like the Sahara, or the Playa del Ingles in Grand Canary. The great problem was what to do? The obvious solution was to plant marram grass, which was easier said than done. In the end, a brushwood thatch was used to contain the sand, and this was then planted with trees. In time, the roots tied the whole mass together, and layers of pine needles helped to produce a sort of soil that encouraged further growth.

It has taken some seventy years to produce the forest that we see today, and it is a magnificent example of land preservation and reclamation. Without it there might have been desert now all the way from Nairn to Forres. Remember this next time the Forestry Commission is getting its usual 'stick'. The forest is an interesting place to visit, and has a very varied and unusual wildlife. There are car parks at Cloddymoss, north of Brodie, and by Wellhill Farm, beyond Kintessack.

HOPEMAN - A golden past and a new town

The coast road runs west from Lossiemouth as straight as a Roman road for several miles. There are cool pinewoods beyond Covesea, and the Laich of Moray stretches away endlessly, to the south, in patchwork fields of green, gold, and reddish brown. In the distance, the lattice towers of the radio station masts pierce the sky and locate the ancient port of Burghead.

About three miles east of Burghead on B9012, and to the north of Duffus, the little old village of Hopeman has suffered a population explosion, and it is fast being embedded in a rash of new housing. Fortunately, the original village is still virtually intact, and an appealing harbour and a wonderful local coastline add to its obvious attractions.

Hopeman was built in 1805 by William Young, a Burghead man, notorious for master-minding the Highland clearances. Its original trade was the export of building stone from the local quarries - a sandstone of fine grain and a beautiful golden hue - and it is still in great demand. In time Hopeman developed into a fishing port which, in common with its more illustrious neighbours, had its greatest prosperity a hundred years ago. The harbour, which was built in the 1830's, is now the haunt of pleasure craft, but a number of the old buildings and businesses remain, and it has an antique air. There is a wonderful and colourful little Victorian crane by the quayside.

Apparently remote and secluded, it is, surprisingly, a most convenient centre for the main attractions and resorts in the Laich of Moray. The magnificent beaches and safe bathing here, on either side of the harbour, and the many secluded coves and caves, all help to make this a deservedly popular little resort. Beach fishing is also good, and boat trips can be arranged. The many amenities include a caravan site, and yet another delightful golf links, which extends to the east atop the old raised beach.

LOSSIEMOUTH - Sand, seaside and the Normans

It has to be said that few people would put Lossiemouth at the top of a list of north-east Scottish seaside resorts. At first sight it is a very ordinary place of recent build, and with the disadvantage of a military airfield close by it may be wondered why people holiday here at all. Once into the town, the old harbour at Branderburgh, and the fabulous beaches and sandhills explain it all. It is then easy to see why this place - big by local standards - is a popular, but not too popular, resort.

The town grew as an amalgam of three old hamlets, and the harbour, with its long breakwater, is actually the third to be built. The medieval port was at Spynie, in a loch that was originally an arm of the sea extending west to Burghead Bay. The river ran out to the north through the loch. By the end of the Middle ages a sandbar had formed at Roseisle, the loch was fast silting up, and the old port became practically unusable. Later, the loch was drained, and in the 17th Cent. a new harbour was constructed at Lossie-Head as the port for Elgin.

Elgin town council at the time spent a lot of money on the project, and even put a local tax on beer to help with the finance. The new port was at present-day Seatown, and it is to be hoped that they were satisfied with what they got. The latest harbour at Branderburgh, with its big stone warehouses, dates from the 1840's and is very picturesque. The colourful small motor fishing vessels and other craft, bobbing up and down on a blue-painted sea, provide the endless fascination common to all small seaports.

Lossiemouth has for long held an important place in Scottish fishing history, and was an innovator of many fishing techniques. It is still a busy and apparently prosperous little port, and it seems to concentrate on inshore fishing nowadays. The fishing industry has always had to adapt or die, and having moved from herring on to net and line fishing for haddock and other white fish, shellfish have been the most recent enterprise.

Ramsay MacDonald was the first Labour Prime Minister of Britain, and he is Lossiemouth's most famous son. Born in Seatown in 1866, his home was at 1, Gregory Place, and the house is now marked by a plaque of Hopeman stone. The Fisheries & Community Museum in Pitgaveny Street, by the harbour, is open on summer weekdays. It has a representation of Ramsay MacDonald's study, and there is an interesting display of the local fishing industry.

The road north from Elgin crosses the old loch bed, which is now a stretch of highly productive farmland. It is very low lying, and there is a noticable climb up to Lossiemouth, which is built on and around Coulard Hill. The coastline to the west is an old raised beach, and the fields fall away steeply to the south.

This is a delightful stretch of seaside, and in addition to the fabulous beaches there are cliffs with coves and caves not far to the west. At Covesea, from beyond a caravan park, the white tower of the lighthouse, rising from the white sands and blue sea, seems more appropriate to the Mediterranean than the Moray Firth. The so called Smugglers Caves that look out to the Skerries have yielded Roman remains. To the east, across the little footbridge over the Lossie, the stretch of glorious beach, sand dunes and woodland is an interesting wildlife habitat that stretches for eight miles all the way to Kingston.

Lossiemouth has all the comforts, conveniences and amenities of a substantial town, and these are combined with the interest and down-to-earth bustle of an old but active fishing harbour. Throw in the river and the varied water sports, fishing in the sea and fifteen miles of river; then add the two golf links, and the delightful beaches and sand hills on either side, and there are all the ingredients for a wonderful holiday.

There are many interesting things to see in the local countryside, and Duffus Castle, a few miles to the south-west, comes as a complete surprise. This ruined 14th Cent. stronghold standing on top of a great Norman motte, and with an encircling moat, is not at all the sort of castle normally associated with Scotland. The finest castle of its type in the north, and the only one in Scotland with a moat, it was originally the seat of the Morays, now represented by the Dukes of Atholl and Sutherland.

At Duffus village, to the north, the ruined old church has a 14th Cent. porch, an interesting churchyard and an old cross shaft which are listed as ancient monuments. Nearby Gordonstoun is the famous school which numbers the Prince of Wales and the Duke of Edinburgh amongst its former pupils. The school was founded in the 1930's, and occupies an ancient house.

It was built between 1650 and 1700 by Sir Robert Gordon, the 'Wizard of Gordonstoun', and in the early 19th Cent. it passed to Sir William Cumming of Altyre, a descendant of the Comyns. In 1809 it was unoccupied, with the furniture piled up in the large deserted rooms. Elizabeth Grant described it as '...like the side of a square in a town for extent and facade.' She wondered what could be done with it.

Whilst at Duffus, Miss Grant lamented that Sir William had '.....had to add the Southron Gordon to the Wolf of Badenoch's long famed name..'. This is an interesting if somewhat inaccurate comment, for it illustrates the strong sense of Celtic heritage and the long, long memory of the Highlander. The Gordons and Comyns were ancient adversaries, and they were, indeed, Southrons, having come to the area in the Norman era. The Gordons were also opposed by the Celtic Stewarts and Grants, and the Wolf of Badenoch was a Stewart.

It must be understood that there was no Norman Conquest of

Scotland; instead there was a gradual infiltration. At the invitation of the 12th Cent. King David I and some of his successors, many Anglo-Normans settled in Galloway, the Lowlands, and the north-eastern coastal plain. They then proceeded to acquire often vast estates by obtaining gifts from the King, or by marrying into wealthy local families - which is precisely what the Comyns and the Gordons did, although the Comyns lost favour during the reign of Robert the Bruce, and most of their estates were given to the Stewarts.

Everywhere the Normans went the feudal system followed, and it was much more rigid and severe than the Celtic clan system. Naturally, they were resented by the locals, and Elizabeth Grant's comment is an echo of an antipathy that had lasted for 600 years!

It is also not uncommon in the Highlands to hear people discussing who did this, or didn't do that, during the '45. What is remarkable is that these things are often discussed as though they had happened only yesterday! So be warned: the Speyside locals are friendly, generally helpful, and quite charming to visitors, and there is no animosity at all to the English. But it obviously is unwise to cross the Highlanders: they have long memories!

NAIRN - The longest town in the country

However unlikely it may seem today, Nairn is a town with a long, if not particularly distinguished, history. The first charter is said to have been granted by Alexander I, which would have been about 1110 AD, and William the Lion built a castle here some fifty years after that. As would be expected, the town was originally built along the river bank, and there are two parts, separated by the bridge: the old town to the south, and Fishertown, downstream towards the sea.

'Old' is relative, for the castle has gone and there are few ancient buildings in the town other than a fine 18th Cent. Court House, and an old cross in High Street. Much of Nairn was rebuilt in the 19th Cent., and the town has an air of solid Victorian comfort and respectability. This was also a period of rapid growth, and it was at this time that Nairn turned into a popular holiday resort, with many hotels and boarding houses built between the old town and the seaside links.

Fishertown extends northwards, between the bridge and the harbour. Separated from the eastern ports by the great sands and dunes along the coast, it is quite unlike the other fishing towns of the Moray Firth. Little terraces of little houses with little gardens stand back-to-back. Their inhabitants were different, too, being of mainly Norse descent, and speaking English instead of Gaelic. The old harbour was extensively rebuilt, first by Telford, and again after suffering severe damage in the flood of 1829. It remains a fascinating place, although the main occupants today are pleasure craft.

Nairn has all the amenities of a large holiday town, including two delightful museums. The Fishertown museum, in King Street, deals with the fishing industry. The Nairn Museum, in Viewfield House at the other end of King Street, is concerned with local history, and has a display and relics of Culloden.

King James VI (I of England) had a decidedly odd sense of humour, and it seems that he really liked to tease the English. On his journey back to England in 1617, he stopped at Kendal and scandalised the whole of Westmorland by knighting two kitchen hands. Some time later he stayed at Hoghton Tower, in Lancashire. At dinner he took Sir Cuthbert's sword and bestowed the accolade upon a roast of beef, and *surloin* has been Sir-loin ever since. In Nairn, the town cross was said to mark the boundary between the Highlands and the Lowlands, and King James once remarked that he had a town with a street so long that the inhabitants at one end could not understand the speech of the people at the other. What he said was true, for Gaelic was spoken in Nairn and English in Fishertown.

Defoe didn't comment on the language, but he had much to say about the countryside, which he considered rich, fruitful and pleasant. This also explains why so many castles and magnificent houses were built in the Laich. Near to Nairn, for example, there are Finlay (broch), Rait (ruin), Cawdor, Kilravock, Dalcross, and Castle Stuart, and they are all worth seeing.

CLAVA, CAWDOR & CULLODEN - far off things & a battle long ago

It should be obvious by now why the Bronze Age Beaker people chose to settle here, and their great ring-cairns and burial chambers at Balnuaran of Clava are superb examples of their kind. In a quiet and lovely little wooded dell, just across the river to the south of B9006, and not far from Culloden, this remarkable group of three megaliths and passage graves - each one different from the others - is, perhaps, the finest in Great Britain. Many of the stones bear cup marks, which seem to be common down the length of eastern Britain, and are thought to be the trade mark of a people who came from Spain some 4000 years ago.

Down a byway off B9090, about five miles from Nairn, Cawdor Castle has been here for some 600 years, and there is a tradition that its site was chosen by a donkey. According to this story, when he decided to build, the thane was instructed in a dream to put all his treasure onto a donkey's back and turn it loose. He was to follow and build where it stopped to rest. He did so, and the animal lay down beside a hawthorn; and this is where the castle was built. In the central tower's undercroft there is a thorn tree trunk which has been carbon dated 1372.

The great 15th Cent. central tower was erected by William, the 3rd Thane, on and around the original 14th Cent. tower. The castle has been regularly extended, altered and modernised, but most of the present fabric is 17th Cent. The castle is open to the public, who

CAWDOR.

enter via a drawbridge across the moat. The great iron yett behind the doors is said to have been carried from Lochindorb when that castle was dismantled on the orders of James II.

At the end of the 15th Cent., by a series of stratagems and accidents that would have made Machiavelli weep, Cawdor passed to the Campbells and has remained in the family ever since. The present Earl has done much to enhance the interior and exterior of the castle, and it is a delightful place to visit.

There are old dungeons and kitchens, with all the equipment of their day. There are more modern rooms with beautiful furniture and fine paintings, not all of them old. It is a rare pleasure to see the works of modern artists like Dali, John Piper and John Glashan juxtaposed with 18th Cent. portraits. There are many other interesting things, and on a grand piano in one room there is a splendid 'B' type beaker from a Bronze Age cist burial. The gardens are a delight, particularly the flower garden by the castle walls. The extensive well-wooded parkland contains nature trails, a picnic area, tea rooms, pitch and putt and many other attractions. The gift shop is superb. Not a place to visit in a hurry, Cawdor is ideal for a day or half-day out. It is also a place where you should take time to read the captions and labels on the many various exhibits. The present Thane wrote them, and they display a sense of sardonic humour which is very refreshing.

Fought in 1746, on what was known then as Drummossie Moor, the Battle of Culloden was the last disaster of the Jacobite cause. On this great lowland plain, a few miles from Nairn on B9006, a force of 5000 tired Highlanders was defeated by 9000 Hanoverian troops commanded by the Duke of Cumberland. It might have been a different story somewhere else - say in the hills, which was the Highlanders' normal battle ground. But on this bare heath, confronted by superior numbers and murderous artillery, they had little chance, and Prince Charles lost a third of his force against Cumberland's 300 casualties.

Culloden is now the haunt of tourists, and is administered by the Scottish National Trust. Tidied-up, and interpreted in the Visitor Centre and museum - Old Leanach farm at the time of the battle - it is one of the most poignant and moving places in Scotland. The Well of the Dead was blocked by bodies after the battle; it still has water, but by tradition no one drinks there now. Little mounds, each one marked by a named stone, identify the resting places of the butchered clansmen, and no visitor can be unaffected by the air of sadness that pervades this site.

The Rose family owned and lived in Kilravock Castle for over 500 years, and entertained Bonnie Prince Charlie on the eve of Culloden. When he arrived next day, the Duke of Cumberland treated the laird with uncharacteristic clemency, and told him that he could not have refused hospitality to a prince. About two miles from Cawdor on the B9091, this magnificent castle dates from the 15th Cent., and the original tower house, built in 1460, was subsequently expanded in the 16th and 18th Cents. Further alterations were made about sixty years ago. The grounds are open on weekdays, and there are castle tours on Wednesdays.

INVERNESS - ancient & elegant capital of the Highlands

The origins of the city are lost in the mists of time, and there are few relics of the past. Tradition has it that St. Columba came here in the 6th Cent. and converted the Pictish king Brude, whose castle may have been the vitrified broch on Craig Phadraig. Macbeth, too, is supposed to have had his castle here, on the eastern side of the present city, but no traces remain, and Auld Castle Road is the only reminder of its existence. The great castle that overlooks the river and dominates the city from the mound of Castle Hill is Victorian. It was built on the site of the old fort that was demolished in the '45.

When Daniel Defoe arrived, shortly after the Jacobite rising of 1715, he was most impressed by the strategic importance of the town's location. So much so, in fact, that he had virtually nothing to say about the town itself. When Boswell arrived with Dr. Johnson in 1773 he was concerned mainly with their stomachs and their lodgings, and he, too, said little about the town. All of which is unfortunate, because virtually every remnant of the past was swept away in a great wave of Victorian rebuilding.

Despite its comparative youth, the modern city has great elegance and charm, and a definite air of antiquity. This could have something to do with the architecture of the Victorians, who were fond of classical themes, and the facades of the buildings in the city centre are a never-ending source of pleasure - look up, above the shop fronts. Displayed here there is every whim and fancy of Victorian architectural taste. Styles range from the classic simplicity of ancient Greece to Rococo fancy and the High Baroque. There is exuberance, extravagance and opulence on the streets, but never a hint of vulgarity. It is all very much in keeping with the prim and proper *persona* of this nice, and rather maiden-auntish gem of a city, and it makes a refreshing change from the glut of Georgiana elsewhere. There is a fine museum by the Castle.

Inverness is a wonderful place for shopping, and as the main commercial centre of the North it has all the big names and amenities of a large city. It also has a certain provincial charm and many small local businesses. The Market Arcade, opposite Station Square, has a wide variety of shops in a real Victorian shopping mall. The old market within the complex has an intriguing and appetising range of local fare. Venison is now fairly commonplace, but the range of savoury sausages and puddings, mutton pies and local fish border on the unusual. The excellent Tourist Information Centre, the banks, and major department stores are all in the vicinity.

There are some interesting old things, and the National Trust, in Church Street, has its offices in a 16th Cent. house that has some unusual internal features. The NTS shop is open during the summer. The old Mercat Cross, now restored, stands outside the Victorian Town House at the bottom of Bridge Street. The cross stands on the 'Tub Stone', said to have been used as a *dhobi* stone by the local washer-women. The 18th Cent. steeple, nearby, was once the city gaol.

The finest cities always have a riverside location, and the river here presents a noble sight. It does, however, influence the climate, and on the broad pavements of Inverness there is always a certain freshness in the air - on a damp day some might call it raw. Across the river, the fine edifice of the 19th Cent. cathedral of St. Andrew stands on the island between the river and the Caledonian Canal. Ness Walk borders the riverside, and leads to Bught Park and Ness Islands, which offer tranquility and pleasant walks near to the city centre. The ice rink, boating park, and other amusements are all in this part of the city. To the west, by the canal, Tomnahurich Cemetry, of all places, has a delightful little hill from which there are some splendid views. There are pleasant woodland walks on Craig Phadraig, off the little road by the entrance locks of the Caledonian Canal.

Along Shore Street, to the north of the city centre, the Clock Tower is the only remnant of Cromwell's 17th Cent. citadel. The presence of a Cromwellian garrison and their assorted camp followers is supposed to be the source of a particularly 'English' intonation in the local dialect. Defoe noticed this and made the following observation: '.....*at the end of those troublesome days, when the troops on all sides came to be disbanded ... an abundance of the English soldiers settled in this fruitful and cheap part of the country... they left them the English accent upon their tongues, and they preserve it also to this day; for they speak perfect English... some will say that they speak it as well as at London.*'

Inverness has had a turbulent past, and no less than seven forts and castles have been built here during its long history. The Cromwellian fort was razed after the Restoration, and it was originally intended to rebuild on the site in 1746. A new fortification was needed because the original Fort George, built on the site of the old castle, was destroyed by Prince Charles's forces shortly before Culloden.

FORT GEORGE, ARDERSIER - the last
bastion of the North

Fort William was built at Inverlochy in 1692 to emphasise the military presence in the Highlands, and two other forts were built along the Great Glen after the rising of 1715. Fort Augustus, the largest, was established by Wade at the south end of Loch Ness in 1724, and Fort George, the most northerly, was also built by Wade on the site of the old castle in Inverness. Fort Augustus and Fort George were destroyed by the Jacobites, and Fort William came within a hair's breadth of destruction. After this humiliation a show of strength was needed, and it was eventually decided to build the new fort at Ardersier. The site, on an isolated peninsula, was ideal for the purpose, and work started in 1748 to a plan drawn up by William Skinner, the Board of Ordnance Engineer.

The work was carried out by the Adam brothers of Kirkcaldy, whose family firm had completed many Government contracts. This was an enormous undertaking, and the site, of over 40 acres, was the size of a substantial town. Ardersier was isolated, and had poor communications, so nearly everything had to be brought in by sea. A harbour was built, a brickworks set up, and a huge workforce of local labour was employed.

By 1770 the fort had been completed at a cost of roughly £175,000 - a huge sum for those days. It was intended to be the finest and most modern military fortress in the world, and it could

FORT GEORGE
ARDERSIER

support a garrison of 1600 men. It was proof against mortars, cannon, mines and infantry, and was totally impregnable to any contemporary form of attack. Unfortunately, by the time of its completion it was out of date! During its long gestation and construction the world had changed; the Jacobite 'menace' had disappeared for ever, and the new fort was redundant.

The fort, for long the depot of the Queen's Own Highlanders, is well worth an extended visit. The principal entrance, across a drawbridge, leads not to a different world but to a different era, and the initial impact is dramatic to say the least. The enormous scale of the buildings - three-storey barrack blocks around a vast square, stables and a chapel, and great expanses of verdant lawn - all contribute to an almost unreal sense of theatre. It is like a film set, and a roll of drums and the appearance of an approaching company of Redcoats would occasion no surprise. The entire fort, with its displays, exhibitions and museum is a spellbinding place in a glorious situation. It is incredible that it is not better known and more often visited.

The approach to the fort from Inverness is by the B9039 Airport Road. Near the junction with A96, picturesque Castle Stuart was once the seat of the Earls of Moray - descendants of Macbeth.

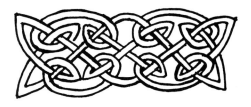

BIRDS & BIRD-WATCHING

Bird watching is a popular pastime. It costs little; it provides a good reason for visiting all sorts of interesting and beautiful places; and the birds themselves can be fascinating creatures. Speyside is an ideal place in which to pursue the activity, but its merits in this respect have been rather obscured by the attention devoted to one particular species.

Almost everyone in Britain must know by now that Loch Garten is the place to go to see an **osprey**. It also seems that, for most people, that is the sum total of all they know about the birds of Speyside. If true, it is unfortunate, for there are many other birds that are just as interesting as the ospreys, even if they are not as spectacular. In the pine woods around Loch Garten, for instance, visitors might reasonably expect to see **crested tits, crossbills and capercailles**, none of which can be regarded as commonplace elsewhere.

Bird life is greatly influenced by geography, and there is consequently an incredible variety of habitats in Spey Valley. They range from sub-arctic tundra, through large areas of coniferous forest and birch scrub, to water-meadow and fen, and the number and variety of species reflect this range. Unfortunately, the veritable surfeit of riches in Spey Valley tends to make the rest of Speyside seem quite tame. Of course, it is not: as John Donne said, comparisons are odious, and there are interesting birds to be seen throughout the area.

Ospreys get the best press, but few people realise that the Scottish osprey population is now well into three figures. Loch

Garten is the honey pot, but there are ospreys everywhere. There are now many nesting sites in Speyside, and these beautiful birds can be seen fishing rivers and lochs almost anywhere between Tugnet, on the Spey estuary, and Spey Dam, not far from the source. The west end of Loch Morlich is a popular spot.

Golden eagles are rare, and if there seem to be no signs of increasing numbers, despite increased protection, remember that eagles need a lot of room - typically some 200 square miles. From the observers' point of view they will never be abundant. Also, they don't care for the presence of people - who can blame them? - so they tend to live in out of the way places. Known Speyside ranges are Abernethy, Lairig Ghru, Glen Feshie, and the upper reaches of the Calder, behind Newtonmore.

Peregrines are exciting birds, and seem to be quite numerous on Speyside. In spring, the raucous cry of a nesting falcon can be heard from many crags. Again, Spey Valley has the most, although birds are present elsewhere on the Spey. One nesting site on Craigellachie, behind Aviemore, has been used regularly for many years, and more birds are present in Strath Nethy.

Sparrowhawks, hen harriers and other birds of prey are regularly seen here, particularly over the Insh Marshes, and **buzzards** will be seen wheeling above the woods and mountains all over Speyside.

Many interesting water fowl are to be seen, including **whooper swans, teal, mallard, and tufted duck**. Many sea ducks may be observed around the Spey estuary. At certain times of the year **goldeneye and wigeon** can seem commonplace on lochs throughout Speyside, as does the **goosander**.

Upland birds are well represented, and the marshy area of the Cairngorm plateau is a noted locality for **dotterel**, which have also been observed on low ground in the vicinity of Abernethy. This delightful bird is also present in the Monadhliaths. **Snow bunting** are found in many of the high mountain areas, as are **ring ouzel and**

ptarmigan. Ptarmigan are quite common above 3000 feet, and it is not necessary to move far from the top station of the Cairngorm chairlift to see some of these high mountain grouse.

The taxonomists have recently burdened us with new names for many familiar Speyside birds. Indeed, it sometimes seems that they indulge in this often irritating activity to ensure a continued need for taxonomists! Why cannot they leave the established species alone, and concentrate on the many new species still awaiting classification and naming? So far as this book is concerned, **red grouse** remain red grouse, and they are fairly plentiful lower down, although populations vary for many different reasons.

Those woodland-dwelling members of the grouse family, **black grouse** and **capercaille**, are present in conifer woodland throughout Speyside. Due to habitat destruction, black grouse are not as numerous as in days gone by but, as a sort of compensation, capercaille numbers seem to be increasing. The Culbin Forest, in Laich of Moray, is a prime locality for woodland birds, as are Rothiemurchus and Abernethy. The woods of Cawdor, and the Findhorn about Sluie are also worthy of attention. **Crossbills, crested, coal** and **long tailed tits**, and **siskins** are some of the other delightful birds of the Speyside woodlands.

Around the moors and coasts there are many different kinds of waders to be seen. **Plovers - ringed and golden, phalaropes, stints, greenshank and redshank, oystercatcher, snipe and woodcock**, for example, are all to be found here, and sea birds abound on the Speyside coast of the Moray Firth. Apart from the sea ducks and waders already mentioned, there are notable colonies of **terns** at various locations.

RECOMMENDED HABITATS

Abernethy & Loch Garten. Ben Aigan. Braes of Glenlivet. Cairngorm plateau. Culbin Forest. Dava Moor. Insh Marshes. Lein - Kingston. Monadhliaths. Roseisle Forest & Burghead Bay. Rothiemurchus. Ryvoan. Speymouth Forest. Whiteness Head - Nairn.

HISTORIC BUILDINGS & ANTIQUITIES

SPEY VALLEY:

Aviemore Stone Circle, Aviemore - Bronze Age circle now landscaped into a housing development opposite the Health Centre.

Castle Grant, Grantown on Spey - originally the seat of the Chief of Clan Grant, and dating from 15th Cent. Subsequently altered, & extended by Robert Adam. Likened to a factory by Queen Victoria. Now undergoing restoration - may soon be open again.

Castle Roy, Nethybridge - remains of small 13th Cent. courtyard castle by B970 north of village. Not open - unsafe.

Dalfour Stone Circle, large Bronze age ring cairn on Alvie estate between Easter & Wester Delfour, 2 miles N. of Kincraig. Ask at Alvie estate office.

Doune House, Rothiemurchus - 16th Cent. home of Grants of Rothiemurchus. Undergoing restoration. Monday afternoon by appointment only. Details from Ranger Centre, Inverdruie.

Insh Church, Kincraig - 7th Cent. foundation on a pagan site. Missionary bell of 10th Cent. and an ancient font.

Ruthven Barracks, Kingussie - splendid 18th Cent. military barracks burnt by the Jacobites in 1746. The '45' rebellion ended here.

STRATHSPEY:

Auchindoun Castle, Dufftown - 15th Cent. stronghold of the Ogilvies built on site of old hill fort. Burnt by the Macintoshes in the 16th Cent. Can be seen from the road: not open - unsafe.

Ballindalloch Castle, Ballindalloch - enormous 16th Cent.

castle of the Macpherson Grants. Open Sunday afternoons in summer.

Balvenie Castle, Dufftown - mammoth 13th Cent. castle of the Atholl Stewarts that has housed Edward I & Queen Mary. Abandoned by the Government after Culloden. Open April - September. Closed Sunday.

Drummuir Castle, Dufftown - 19th Cent. Gothick home of the Gordon Duff family. Open on Sunday afternoons in summer.

Lecht Mine, Nr. Tomintoul - repaired crushing mill building by picnic area at **Well of the Lecht**, 6 miles south of Tomintoul.

Mill of Towie, Nr. Keith - 19th Cent. watermill producing oatmeal for Drummuir Castle estate. Genuine & very interesting.

Mortlach Church, Dufftown - much restored church built on site dating back to 6th Cent. Notable for its Pictish cross & other monuments.

Rothes Castle, Rothes - fragment of 12th/13th Cent. castle of the Leslies. Occupied until 17th Cent., & later destroyed by townsfolk.

SPEYMOUTH:

Coxton Tower, Lhanbryde - picturesque white harled 17th Cent. tower house by B9103. Can be seen from road: not open.

Cullen Auld Kirk, Nr. Cullen - 14th Cent. church with notable gallery & monuments.

Cullen House, Cullen - early 17th Cent. house owned by the Seafield Estate. Grounds open Tuesday & Friday afternoons.

Findlater Castle, Cullen - ruined 15th Cent. castle on clifftop east of Cullen. Structure unsafe.

Gollachy Ice-House, on shore road between Portgordon & Buckie - restored 19th Cent. ice-house contemporary with Tugnet.

Innes House, Nr. Garmouth - 18th Cent. home of the Tennant's. Gardens open weekdays April - July.

Tugnet Ice-House, Spey Bay - built 1830 for Spey salmon

fishery. Now an exhibiton & visitor centre open June - September.

LAICH OF MORAY:

Birnie Kirk, Nr. Elgin - delightful 12th Cent. Norman church.

Braco's Banking House, Elgin - picturesque 17th Cent. piazza house at east end of High Street. Piazza converted into a cycle shop.

Brodie Castle, Nr. Forres - splendid castle comprising 16th Cent. tower house with 17th Cent. & more recent additions. Splendid interior, paintings & furnishings. NTS: open April - September.

Cawdor Castle, Cawdor, Nr. Nairn - magnificent fortified house of various periods from 14th Cent.

Clava Ring Cairns, Culloden - three different types of Bronze Age cairns and passage graves; cup marked stones; well preserved.

Dallas Dhu Distillery, Nr. Forres - Old distillery now used as whisky industry exhibition centre. Open April - September.

Duffus Castle, Nr. Lossiemouth - incredible ruined Norman castle on a great mound surrounded by a water-filled moat.

Elgin Cathedral - originally built in 13th Cent., burnt by 'Wolf of Badenoch', rebuilt but now ruined. Magnificent in its fabric and setting, and with interesting tombs.

Kilravock Castle, Croy, Nr. Nairn - 15th c. tower house with more recent additions & alterations. Open Wednesdays May - September.

Old Mills, Elgin - restored water mill. Open Tuesday - Sunday, April - October.

Pluscarden Abbey, Nr. Forres - dating from 13th Cent. and occupied by Benedictines since 1948, restoration of the abbey continues.

Rodney Stone, Nr. Forres - Pictish symbol stone by entrance drive of Brodie Castle. April - September.

St. Aethan's Well, Burghead - early Christian baptistry (?)

within remains of Iron age fort.

Sueno's Stone, Forres - unique 9th/10th Cent. monolith with relief carving thought to depict victory over the Vikings.

INVERNESS:

Castle Stuart, Nr. Inverness - picturesque 17th Cent. home of the Earls of Moray, undergoing restoration. On airport road near to Culloden. Open May - October.

Craig Phadraig, Inverness - Pictish broch on wooded hill two miles north-west of the city centre.

Fort George, Ardersier - the ultimate 18th Cent. military fortress with Adam associations.

Lochindorb Castle, Dava Moor - ruined 13th Cent. castle on an island was the sequestered 14th Cent. seat of Alexander Stewart - 'Wolf of Badenoch'. The great yett, or gate, is at Cawdor.

FISHING ON SPEYSIDE

The Spey is one of the supreme salmon rivers of the world, and a chance to wet a line in its racing waters must be high up on the wish-list of every visiting game-fisherman. It is not an impossible dream. Fishing on the lower reaches, below Grantown, is exclusive to say the least, and although some fishing is available here to residents of certain hotels, it tends to be quite expensive. It is a rather different story above Grantown, and some associations open their waters to visitors staying in the area. This fishing is often very good. It is also encouraging to note that (in 1992) sea trout are running well again after a mysterious decline. Good fish are landed as far upstream as Newtonmore in May.

The turbulent and scenic Findhorn and the Nairn are also highly rated and, again, some stretches are open to visitors. Also of interest to the tourist is the worthwhile fishing to be had in lesser rivers, streams and lochs throughout Speyside. Loch Insh, a widening of the Spey near Kingussie, contains char. The usual (English) method of fishing for this Ice-Age relic is deep spinning near the bottom from a boat. Char are worth catching, for they are probably the finest flavoured of all game fish.

Once upon a time, not all that long ago, brown trout fishing was usually free. Those days have gone, but on some lochs where they are the only game fish the sport is still amazingly cheap. There are plenty of fisheries, and although the wild trout do not grow very big in the acid waters of the local lochs, their violence more than compensates for lack of size. The settings of the lochs are often just as wild as the fish. Embowered by heathery moors or gentle hills, trout fishing in these surroundings is the perfect antidote to a frantic world, and a delightful day is guaranteed. An immense amount of pleasure is to be had just from being in such beautiful countryside. Sea fishing from shore and boat is generally good, and cod, pollack, other white fish, and mackerel abound. The mouth of the Lossie, and the Spey from Kingston Beach, also provide exciting shore fishing in the breakers for sea trout swimming down the coast to the river estuaries.

Coarse fishing is not a sport with any local following on Speyside, but visiting pike specialists have been known to become quite excited by the possibilities of certain Spey Valley lochs. Twelve pound fish are quite commonplace, and they certainly run up to thirty pounds in some waters. The fishing seasons are generally February - September for salmon, April - September for trout, and all year round for pike, and for rainbow trout in specialist fisheries. There are local variations, so always ask.

An NRA rod licence is not needed when fishing in Scotland, but local permits are essential, and must be obtained before starting to fish. This is most important, for poaching is not a trivial offence, and fishing without a permit is poaching. Note that permits are needed for sea fishing in some places. Also note that fishing is sometimes available only to visitors staying in the locality to be fished. Tourist Information Offices are a mine of information on local fishing, which is often not advertised. Speyside permits, and full information about local fishing may be obtained from the following:

SPEY VALLEY

Aviemore - Mrs Cook, Avielochan - Avielochan & Loch Vaa.

Rothiemurchus Farm Shop, Inverdruie - Rivers Druie & Spey, Lochs Pityoulish (big pike); & fish farm for rainbows all year.

Glenmore Camp Site Warden - Loch Morlich (big pike), and Queen's Forest burns.

Boat of Garten - Allen's Store, Deshar Road; local hotels -

Abernethy Angling Association waters on rivers Spey, Nethy, & some local lochs.

Dalwhinnie - Loch Ericht Hotel - Loch Ericht; other local waters.

Grantown on Spey - C. G. Mortimer, 61 High Street; Angus Stuart, 60 High Street; Seafield hotel - Strathspey Angling Association waters on rivers Spey & Dulnain, Avielochan, Lochindorb, Lochs Dallas, Mhor, Vaa. (Note: Arthur Oglesby teaches here).

Kincraig - Alvie Estate Office & Dalraddy Caravan Park - rivers Spey & Feshie, Lochs Alvie (big pike) & Insh.

Loch Insh Watersports - Loch Insh.

Kingussie - The Paper Shop, King Street; Spey Tackle, High Street - Badenoch Angling Association waters rivers Calder, Spey, Truim Tromie; Spey Dam, Lochs Ericht, Laggan, Uvie. Loch Gynack.

Laggan - Laggan Stores - Spey Dam.

Nethybridge - Allens Stores, Boat of Garten; C. G. Mortimer, High Street, Grantown; local hotels - Abernethy & Strathspey Angling Associations waters on rivers Dulnain, Nethy, Spey & local lochs.

Newtonmore - Ashdown Stores - Badenoch Angling Association waters rivers Calder, Spey, Truim & Tromie; Spey Dam, & Lochs Ericht, Laggan & Uvie.

STRATHSPEY

(Charlestown of) Aberlour - J. A. Munro, 93 High Street (opposite The Square); local hotels - River Spey.

Ballindalloch - Ballindalloch Estate Office; Delnashaugh Hotel, on A95 - River Avon.

Craigellachie - Craigellachie Hotel - River Spey and other lesser local waters. Check availability prior to booking.

Dufftown - J. Rutherford, Conval Street; TV Services, The Square - rivers Dullan & Fiddich.

Keith - Drummuir Estate Office, Drummuir - Loch Park, Drummuir. FREE trout fishing - River Isla, Grange.

Tomintoul - The Post Office, The Square; local hotels - rivers Avon, Conglass & Livet.

SPEYMOUTH

Buckie - Slater Sports, High Street: advice etc. - sea fishing.

Cullen - Seafield Estates Office, York Place - Boyne & Cullen Burns.

Fochabers - Gordon Arms Hotel residents - River Spey.

Kingston - Garmouth Post Office - beach fishing for sea trout.

Lhanbryde - D. Kinloch, Keepers Cottage, B9130 - Loch na Bo.

LAICH OF MORAY

Elgin - Angling Centre, Moss Street; The Tackle shop, 188 High Street - River Lossie, & Lossiemouth Beach (sea trout).

Millbuies Country Park Warden - Millbuies Loch & Glenlatterach Reservoir.

Findhorn - Moray Watersports, Old Fisheries - Findhorn estuary.

Forres - Tackle Shop, 97 High Street - Loch of the Blairs, Lochindorb, Muckle Burn.

Lossiemouth - Homecrafts, 16 Queen Street - River Lossie.

Nairn - P. Fraser, 41 High Street - Nairn Angling Association water: lower reaches to sea. Sea fishing from harbour. General Stores, 19 Harbour Street - Clunas Dam; Clava Lodge Holiday Homes, Culloden Moor - River Nairn.

INVERNESS

Inverness - Tourist Information Centre, 23 Church Street; Grahams, 37 Castle Street; M. Jamieson, 58 Church Street - River Ness. FREE brown trout fishing in River Foyers: B852 on eastern side of Loch Ness.

GARDENS, NURSERIES & GARDEN CENTRES

Notable gardens are not a feature of the more mountainous parts of Speyside or of Strathspey. Most of those that do exist are not open to the public. The balance is redressed a little in the lowland area to the north, where some of the old castles and houses have gardens and parks in keeping with their status.

SPEY VALLEY

Castle Grant, Grantown on Spey - undulating parkland with fine avenue of limes, and many other trees. Worth visiting for the views alone. May open after castle restoration.

Jack Drake, Inshriach - on B970, between Inverdruie & Feshiebridge, this is one of Britain's finest alpine nurseries. Fabulous alpine and other flowers, trees & shrubs in a delightful garden setting. Plantsmen will spend a lot of time here.

Speyside Heather Garden Centre, Skye of Curr, Dulnain Bridge - signposted, just off A95, this specialist nursery concentrates on ericaceous plants, with a few house plants in the gift shop. Nice garden and tea rooms.

Woodcliffe Nursery, Newtonmore - a wide range of plants is available from this new nursery on Laggan Road, at the edge of the village. Limited opening in winter.

STRATHSPEY

Ballindalloch Castle, A95 between Grantown & Aberlour - grounds open Sunday afternoons. Wonderful spring bulbs.

Drummuir Castle, Nr. Keith - huge walled kitchen garden, totally organic, is worth visiting. Open Sun/Wed/Thurs/Fri afternoons.

SPEYMOUTH

Christies Nurseries, Fochabers - large garden centre with noted floral clock & tea rooms.

Cullen House, Nr. Cullen - grounds open Tuesday & Friday afternoons.

Innes House, Nr. Kingston - attractive formal gardens with herbaceous borders & unusual shrubs and trees. Walled garden. Open April - July, Monday - Friday.

LAICH OF MORAY

Brodie Castle, Nr Forres - NTS maintain a marvellous Victorian wild garden here. There are interesting trees and shrubs, and the grounds are noted for their daffodils.

Cawdor Castle, on B9090 near to Culloden - delightful formal flower garden and a splendid wild garden that is at its best in late spring. Open May - October.

Kilravock Castle, off B9091 nr. Croy - extensive parkland with many large and unusual trees. Grounds include nature trails and a beautiful stretch of river. Open May - September.

Kincorth, Nr. Forres - charming old rose garden on west side of Findhorn Bay. Open June - mid-September.

New Fleenas Nursery, on A939 4 miles out of Nairn - small nursery specialising in herbaceous perennials, but with a good selection of other flowers, shrubs & trees.

GOLF - a great Scottish game

It is hardly surprising that both the oldest golf club in the world and the headquarters of the game are to be found in the country where golf was born. It is also reasonable to say that golf, like game fishing, is something of a national obsession. This being the case, it is also not surprising that Scotland boasts some of the world's finest courses of all types. With some two dozen courses listed here, Speyside has its fair share.

The game of golf is a Scottish invention and, like the national game of shinty, it has ancient roots. Some interesting 14th Cent. Dutch paintings depict people playing a game on ice, in which something that looks very like a shinty stick is used to hit a flat disc at a target. The name of the game was 'kolven', which would have been pronounced 'golfen', so the stick was a golfen club. On the basis of this somewhat dubious evidence it has been claimed that golf was invented by the Dutch. What a load of nonsense: golf isn't played on ice!

There was a lot of to-ing and fro-ing between Scotland and the Low Countries in times gone by, and it is more than likely that some canny Scottish visitors would have seen a game of kolven and said: "We could make a proper game out of this golfen." So the clubs, and therefore the name, were used for the quite different game that was then developed in Scotland.

There is an official reference to the game in 1457 when King James II's Parliament prohibited golf because it was causing serious neglect of the obligatory archery practice. It was '....*decreed and ordained that weapon showings be held by the Lords and Barons spiritual and temporal four times in the year, and that football and golf be utterly cried down and not used.'*

Obviously, the ban didn't work, and it is generally accepted that the modern game comes from Scotland. It was a firmly established national pastime (some might say passion) by the reign of James II, and the first golf 'international' was played at Leith links in 1681. The Duke of York - who became James VII/ II in 1685 - played in a match against two English noblemen who had declared golf to be an English invention. Scotland won.

Nowadays, virtually every Scottish town and village has a golf course nearby. Golf in Scotland is remarkably inexpensive and free from queues, and a warm welcome awaits the visitor at each and every one of Speyside's courses. They range from little nine-holers in the mountains - by no means to be despised, to classic seaside links like Old Nairn and Spey Bay.

In his autobiography Mark Twain wrote: *'a game of golf is a good walk spoiled'*. Quite evidently, he had never played the game on Speyside. However testing they may be, the courses here offer much sheer enjoyment and little agony, and the only real distraction is the scenery.

The casual golfer, looking for a day's relief during a family holiday, will have a course to hand almost anywhere in the region. And the golfer's family will have plenty to occupy them, too.

At the other extreme, hopeless addicts will find here the basis for years of happy holidays, and a further attraction is the Visitors Ticket scheme operated in various localities. In Moray, for instance, the five-day ticket provides the run of ten different courses between Monday and Friday in any single week between April and October. At around £50 this is, surely, an offer that no golfer can refuse.

Moray visitor tickets are valid at the golf clubs asterisked (*) in the following list, and they can be bought from any of these clubs, or from the Tourist Information Centres in Buckie, Cullen, Dufftown, Elgin, Forres, Lossiemouth and Keith.

SPEYSIDE GOLF COURSES

Abernethy - 0479 82305 9 holes, SSS 33, 2484 yards.

By the side of the B970 at Nethybridge, which is a little downstream from Boat of Garten, this is an enjoyable yet challenging course near the river and by the great pine woods of Abernethy.

Boat of Garten - 0479 83282 18 holes, SSS 68, 5720 yards. Designed by James Braid, and set in the idyllic surroundings of birch woodlands by the Spey, this testing but rewarding course is known as the "Gleneagles of the north" and, as a bonus, it has absolutely stunning views of the Cairngorms.

Buckie, Buckpool - 0542 32236 18 holes, SSS 70, 6257 yds. *

A links course to the west of the town with super views across the Moray Firth in the typically windy conditions of a seaside course. There are no great ups or downs, but the golf is not easy. Advance booking is requested.

Buckie, Strathlene - 0542 31798 18 holes, SSS 69, 5957 yards. *

This course, on the other side of the town, extends almost to Findochty. Of quite a different character to its neighbour, it offers equally testing golf and good views

Carrbridge - 0479 84674 9 holes, SSS 66, 5300 yards (18 holes).

Not to be taken too seriously, this is an ideal place for a light-hearted round in attractive surroundings. Moorland and parkland, and magnificent scenery.

Cullen - 0542 40685 18 holes, SSS 62, 4610 yards. *

The delightful setting by the sea on Cullen Bay, between the beach and the cliffs, provides plenty of distractions from the many hazards of these little links. Laid out on the west side of the town, this is a little course with a big reputation.

Dufftown - 0340 20325 18 holes, SSS 67, 5308 yards. *

Located in Glen Rinnes, about a mile out of town on the Tomintoul road, this hilly moorland course provides testing golf in a wonderful setting. One of the highest golf course in Britain, with one hole well above the 1000 foot contour, there are views of Ben Rinnes, and the nearby ruined Auchindoun Castle,

Elgin - 0343 542338 18 holes, SSS 71, 6401 yards.

At Hardhillock, south of Elgin, this beautiful parkland course won high praise from Peter Alliss. He considers it to be, perhaps, the finest inland course in the north, and the undulating fairways and tight greens command respect.

Forres - 0309 72949 18 holes, SSS 69, 6141 yards. *

A pleasant alternative to the many links in the area, this parkland course with much attractive woodland has tight greens which reward accurate putting. It offers excellent golf to players of all standards.

Garmouth & Kingston - 0343 87388 18 holes, SSS 67, 5649 yards. *

On the west bank of the Spey estuary, and close to the seaside of the Moray Firth, this delightful and intriguing parkland course in a links setting provides some unique challenges.

Grantown on Spey - 0479 2079 18 holes, SSS 67, 5745 yards.

Founded more than 100 years ago, this old course in an old town has something to offer to players of every standard. Although basically a fairly demanding parkland course, the fairways of the middle six holes, in a typical local woodland setting, provide a different set of problems.

Hopeman - 0343 830578 18 holes, SSS 67, 5474 yards. *

On the B9040 on the E. side of the village, this seaside course is locally renowned for its fiendish 148 yard 12th. The golf here is never less than interesting, and can be very testing. If it all becomes too much there are delightful beaches nearby.

Inverness - 0463 239882 18 holes, SSS 70, 6226 yards.

An old championship course in a parkland, easy walking is combined with testing golf, and there are plenty of natural hazards.

Inverness, Torvean - 0463 237543 18 holes, SSS 68, 5451 yards.

By the side of the Caledonian Canal and in a parkland setting, golf here is not too demanding. This municipal course, about a mile out of town on the A82 Fort William road, offers an enjoyable day at an incredibly low price.

Keith - 0542 22469 18 holes, SSS 68, 5767 yards. *

In Fife Park on the south side of Fife Keith, this admirable parkland course has many natural hazards and exemplary greens. A round here will always be enjoyed, and there is magnificent scenery as well.

Kingussie - 0540 661600 18 holes, SSS 67, 5555 yards.

Designed by Harry Vardon, an Open Champion and a legendary golfer of the Victorian era, the course was opened in the 1890's, and has been enchanting golfers ever since. Situated in the foothills of the Monadhliath mountains, the highest green is at 1000 feet, and there are stunning views of the Spey Valley.

Lossiemouth, Moray New - 0343 812018 18 holes, SSS 69, 6005 yards. *

This new course, a typical seaside links on Lossiemouth west beach, provides testing golf in a delightful setting.

Lossiemouth, Moray Old - 0343 812018 18 holes, SSS 72, 6643 yards.

The elder sister of Moray New, designed by Tom Morris and modified by Henry Cotton, this championship course is the epitome of a Scottish links. A real test of golf is leavened by the superb views across the Firth.

Nairn, Dunbar - 0667 52741 18 holes, SSS 71, 6431 yards.

Across the river from Fishertown, on the east side of Nairn, this is one of a trio of links in this famous golfing resort. By no means inferior to the old course, there are some superb long holes and testing golf.

Nairn, Newton - 0667 53208 9 holes, SSS 59, 2035 yards.

A totally different proposition to the adjacent old course, these little links will appeal to casual golfers (if there are such beings), beginners, high handicappers and the aged.

Nairn, Old - 0667 53208 18 holes, SSS 71, 6556 yards.

Andrew Simpson, Tom Morris and James Braid all had a hand in fashioning this famous and demanding championship course with fearsome bunkers. These fine links to the west of the town have the added attraction of wonderful seaside views.

Newtonmore - 0540 673591 18 holes, SSS 68, 5890 yards.

On the old flood plain of the River Spey, where huge cattle fairs were held in days gone by, this parkland course offers a combination of splendid golf amidst splendid scenery.

Rothes - 0340 3443 9 holes, SSS 68 (18 holes), 2526 yards. *

This attractive little course at Blackhall, to the west of the town, is virtually brand new, having been created in 1990 on local upland pasture. Although play here is not too demanding, there is much to satisfy the discerning golfer. The views of Strathspey, down below, are simply glorious.

Spey Bay - 0343 820424 18 holes, SSS 69, 6059 yards. *

On the east side of the Spey estuary, and set immediately behind the mighty shingle banks of Spey Bay, this classic course has all that one expects of a seaside links. The undulating fairways provide testing golf, and the beach and whin are an added trial on some holes.

HIGHLAND GAMES - A very Scottish spectacle.

It must be admitted that, to some, bagpipe music can be something of a trial, and it is usually an acquired taste, but there is no denying that the sound of the pipes cannot be ignored, and they always make the scalp tingle or the hackles rise. Everyone has a mental image of a pipe band, with drums beating, pipes skirling and kilts swirling, parading on the field at a Highland gathering. Despite the splendour of it all, the pageantry can have an almost primitive air, and it is not too difficult to imagine the original purpose of the day.

The origins of the games are lost in the dim and distant mists of time, but they can be traced back to Malcolm IV in 1153, and it is easy to speculate about how they could have developed with the passing of the years. At the approach of autumn, the cattle were brought down from the summer shielings and the oats and barley were gathered in. There would then be some sort of festive gathering at which the Laird would acknowledge his share and receive tributes.

There would be a review of the Laird's retainers and fighting men, and there would be rivalry and wagers, and impromptu contests and shows of strength. There would be feasting, and drinking, and dancing. In time the festivities would grow beyond the immediate locality, and would expand to embrace a whole district, or a particular clan. The pastoral and agricultural aspects would be later diverted into 'harvest homes' elsewhere.

This would have been a brighter side of the old clan system, and, like that system, the games perished in the aftermath of the '45.

-213-

Between 1746 and 1782 it was forbidden to speak Gaelic, to wear Highland dress, or to engage in anything that could be remotely construed as having a connection with Scottish nationalism. So the games were out; and they remained so until their revival at the beginning of the Victorian era.

The present popularity of the games can be traced back to Queen Victoria. The Queen and Prince Albert attended their first meeting on Prince Albert's birthday in August 1847, whilst enjoying a month's holiday in the Highlands. These games were not, as popularly supposed, at Braemar, but at Ardverikie on Loch Laggan, and not a million miles from Laggan Bridge. By the following year the royal couple had acquired Balmoral, and they attended the Braemar gathering at Invercauld. So highland games were 'in' again, and they have remained so ever since.

The Queen enjoyed the gatherings and was most impressed by the immense strength of the competitors in the field events, and she made many references to the games in her journal. Writing of a foot race at Braemar, she described it as '... *a pretty wild sight, but the men looked very cold with their bare legs & nothing on but their shirts & kilts...*' Which, incidentally, seems to provide the answer to an age-old question!

Under royal patronage the Braemar gathering flourished. It is still the biggest and best of the games, and is always graced by the presence of royalty. Other games were started at Dunoon (Cowal), and Oban (Argyll), and the revival quickly spread. The Victorian author Alexander Smith had Sergeant McTurk say something like this about the 'Highland Games, Inverness 1864':

Hurrah for the Highland glory!
Hurrah for the Highland games!
God bless you, noble gentlemen!
God love you, bonny dames!
And sneer not at the brawny limbs,
And the strength of our Highland men -

When the bayonets next are levelled,
They may be needed then.

So the bellicose background had not been forgotten!

The games are always a big social occasion, and a typical gathering will have the local Laird as president, and he will be received with some degree of pageantry and ceremony. There will be field and track events, Highland dancing, and a piping contest. Track events include running, hurdling, jumping and vaulting. The field events are usually the centre of attention, and there is a circuit of famous 'heavies' who go round the games and attract a tremendous following. These events include shot putting, which will have originated as a boulder throwing contest; throwing the hammer, originally, perhaps, contested by smiths - sinewy and extremely strong; and tossing the caber - the highlight of the games for many folk.

'Caber' is Gaelic for a tree, and a caber is a pine tree trunk of some 17 - 20 feet in length, and weighing anything from 90 - 130 pounds. It is lifted vertically, small end down, and thrown to turn from end to end. It must finish flat on the ground with the small end pointing directly away from the thrower. Contrary to popular opinion, a good throw requires a high degree of skill, strength, fitness, and finesse.

Nowadays there are meetings all over Scotland, and not all are in the Highlands. the following games in Speyside vary in size and content, but all guarantee an entertaining and enjoyable day.

SPEYSIDE HIGHLAND GAMES CALENDAR
June
Grange Highland Games, Keith

Grantown on Spey Highland Games
July
Forres Highland Games

Inverness Highland Games

Elgin Highland Games
Tomintoul & Strathavon Highland Games
Dufftown Highland Games
Rothiemurchus International & World
Championship Highland Games - Inverdruie

August
Aberlour & Strathspey Highland Games
Newtonmore Highland Games
Abernethy Highland Games & Clan Grant
Gathering - Nethy Bridge
Nairn Highland Games

Dates vary from year to year, so check locally to see what is on where and when.

MUSEUMS & SOME OTHER EXHIBITIONS

SPEY VALLEY

Aviemore: Visitor Centre, Inverdruie - a small but interesting 'look and feel' display & video presentation of Rothiemurchus.

Boat of Garten: Station - Strathspey Railway memorabilia.

Glenmore: Forestry Enterprise Visitor Centre - a superb audio-visual show about the forest and its inhabitants.

Grantown-on-Spey: Courthouse, The Square - the Heritage Trust usually has a summer exhibition of Grantown & Strathspey.

Kingussie: Highland Folk Museum, Duke Street - a super museum plus many other exhibits & demo's. A wonderful evocation of Highland life. If you can visit only one museum this is it.

Newtonmore: Clan Macpherson Museum, Main Street - a comprehensive and fascinating presentation of everything to do with the clan.

SPEYMOUTH

Buckie: Maritime Museum, Cluny Place - fishing industry museum plus a gallery of excellent local paintings by Peter Anson.

Fochabers: Baxters Visitor Centre - reproduction of original Victorian shop plus factory tour & other attractions.

Fochabers: Folk Museum, High Street - private local history collection of the Christie's & lots of horse drawn vehicles: nicely complements the museum in Kingussie.

Spey Bay: Tugnet Ice House - salmon fisheries & local wildlife exhibition in restored 19th Cent. ice-house. Audio-visual show.

STRATHSPEY

Aberlour: The Village Store, High Street - a delightful collection of bygones from the first half of the 20th Cent., plus an excellent gift shop.

Aberlour: Visitor Centre, High Street - a small but interesting local history exhibition.

Dufftown: The Clock Tower, The Square - A Georgian building, once the town hall & gaol, now the Tourist Information Centre with a small museum of local history & the whisky industry.

Tomintoul: Visitor Centre, The Square - absorbing & informative small museum & exhibition of local history & natural history.

LAICH OF MORAY

Burghead: Archaeological Museum - local history, of which there is plenty, and casts of the famous Pictish Stones.

Elgin: Elgin Museum, High Street - local history & natural history in an interesting building.

Elgin: Moray Motor Museum, Bridge Street - everything to do with motor cars, motorcycles & motoring in bygone days.

Forres: Falconer Museum, Tolbooth Street - museum of local history & natural history.

Forres: Nelson Tower, Cluny Hill - small exhibition of Nelsoniana and a superb viewpoint: worth the climb.

Lossiemouth: Fisheries & Community Museum - local interest museum with a reproduction of Ramsay MacDonald's study: in a converted warehouse by the harbour.

Nairn: Fishertown Museum, King Street - history of local fisheries.

Nairn: Nairn Museum, King Street - local history & relics of Culloden.

Nairn: Highland Railway Museum, Railway Station - a must for all railway buffs.

INVERNESS

Museum & Art Gallery, Castle Wynd - Highland history & natural history plus interesting pictures.

Fort George, Ardersier - Seafield collection of early armaments & Regimental Museum of the Queen's Own Highlanders.

PONY TREKKING & RIDING

Horseback was a normal mode of travel in days gone by, and the highland pony is the result of centuries of selective breeding. With a warm coat impervious to the weather, a sure foot and an even temper, it has long been used to carry people around the hills, and as a 'garron' to bring back the spoils of a day's stalking. Queen Victoria was probably the first person to use a pony to get to noted beauty spots, and ponies were then often used as an alternative to hill walking by 19th Cent. tourists. The coming of the motor car put an end to our familiarity with the horse, and people walked around the hills until a Speyside man, Cameron Ormiston, introduced the pastime of pony trekking in 1951. The sport is firmly established on Speyside, and riding and pony trekking can be enjoyed at many centres.

SPEY VALLEY :

Ballintean Riding Centre, Kincraig - 05404 352.

Carrbridge Trekking Centre, Station Road - 047984 602

Croila Trekking Centre, Newtonmore - 0540 661705

Haflinger Centre, Laggan Rd., Newtonmore - 05403 527

Nethybridge Riding Centre, in village centre - 047982 693

Parks Centre, Kingussie - 0540 661247

STRATHSPEY :

Aberlour Riding & Trekking Centre, Aberlour House - 0340 871467

Drumbain Riding School, Rothes - 03403 250

Knockandhu Riding School, Mulben - 05426 302

Tomintoul Trekking Centre, Argyll House - 08074 223
Ski-Equi Holidays, St. Bridget's Farm, Tomintoul - 08074 221
SPEYMOUTH :
Garmouth Riding Centre, Garmouth - 034387 445
Hazelpark Riding School, Gollachy, Buckie - 0542 31271
Redmoss Riding Centre, Drybridge, Buckie - 0542 33140
LAICH OF MORAY :
Kinloss Riding Stables, Old Schoolhouse, Kinloss - 0309 692218
Logie Farm Riding Centre, Glenferness, Nairn - 0309 651226

WALKS & WALKING

Speyside seems tailor-made for walkers, whatever their requirements may be, and virtually anywhere in the area will make a good base for some sort of walking holiday. Everything from a gentle riverside jaunt to an extended back-packing trek through the wilds can be enjoyed here, and the marked lack of crowds is a great advantage.

Hill walkers are really spoiled for choice, and although most people seem to plump for Spey Valley and the Cairngorms, there are other options to consider. From Dalwhinnie through to Carrbridge, the west side of the Spey is bounded by the Monadhliaths. More than 200 square miles in extent, this is an enormous area of virtually trackless mountains. In total contrast to the Cairngorms, it is a great massif of green and knobbly hills, all somewhere around 2500 feet, with intervening valleys and a myriad streams that feed the Dulnain, the Findhorn and the Spey.

Land Rover tracks have been cut in some places by the big estates, but they are few and far between, and these hills have great potential for experienced lovers of wilderness walking. If access to the Cairngorms is restricted, as the Ramblers Association and some other bodies wish, the Monadhliaths will, undoubtedly, become better known. The easiest access is from Newtonmore and Kingussie, whilst Tomatin is well placed for Strathdearn and the upper Findhorn.

The Hills of Cromdale, between Strathspey and Strath Avon, and the Crown Estate of Glenlivet, north of Tomintoul, offer potentially good hill and moorland walking, especially outside the shooting and stalking seasons. These areas, and the country around Ben Rinnes, should be seriously considered for walking holidays based in Strathspey.

Speymouth and the Laich of Moray are technically lowland, but they are none the worse for that. 'Lowland' does not mean that the country is like a bowling green, and the countryside has considerable attraction and charm. There is great variety here, with a succession of low hills, verdant farms, huge woodlands, and an extensive and seductive shore. Some of the forest walks equal anything to be found elsewhere. The coastal woodlands at Roseisle and Culbin are particularly attractive because they are by the shore. At Roseisle the beach is fringed with Corsican pines. In summer their heady scent hangs heavy in the air, and a stroll here is redolent of the Mediterranean. The best known walk, that starts from Spey Bay, is, of course, the Speyside Way.

THE SPEYSIDE WAY

Long distance paths through river valleys are not new, but they are still quite rare. The first and best was the Dales Way, which starts from Ilkley in Yorkshire, and finishes by Windermere. The Speyside Way was a wonderful idea that didn't quite come off. Originally intended to provide a continuous walking route from Spey Bay to Glenmore, it ran into access problems beyond Ballindalloch, and the purely Speyside section ends there. To provide a more satisfactory end point, an extension was negotiated across the Crown Estate in Glenlivet, and a spur now goes on to Tomintoul, where accommodation and transport are more readily available.

The first section south from Tugnet is mainly pleasant, and fishermans paths are followed nearly all the way to Fochabers. The paths never stray far from the river, and they traverse a delightful mix of pasture, rough scrub and woodland. The next six miles, to Boat of Brigg, can be something of a trial, being mainly on a minor road. But there is little traffic, and at Ordquiesh the Aultdearg earth pillars are really spectacular. The last mile, through Delfur woods, is a happy relief.

From Boat of Brigg to Craigellachie, the route uses Forestry Commission tracks along the flank of Ben Aigan, with the last portion, again, on minor roads. This section of the Way offers some splendid views. The Visitor Centre, by the old station at Fiddich Park, has an interesting little exhibition, a very helpful Warden, and lots of information. A delightful spur goes seven miles on an old rail bed to a finish at Dufftown.

The next bit of the Way, to Ballindalloch, is twelve miles or so of undiluted pleasure along the rail bed of the disused Strathspey line. There are many bosky wildlife havens and all sorts of other interesting things.

The old station at Aberlour has a tea shop, and better still, perhaps, the station of Knockando, attractive in itself, was turned into the Visitor Centre for the Tamdhu distillery. Allow plenty of time, and enjoy the free dram. The Way, as such, ends at the car park in the old Ballindalloch station yard.

Ballindalloch is an inconvenient place to finish, but a bus goes to Tomintoul at 5.30 pm on three days a week. If walking the entire Way, a spur follows mainly hill and moorland tracks for fifteen miles to Tomintoul. Glenlivet is at the mid-point of this section, and the last few miles of the route traverse Cairn Daimh (1900 ft.), and then a stretch of bog just above Tomintoul.

Seasoned back-packers, keen to carry on to Glenmore, can follow the old track from Bridge of Brown, via Dorback Lodge, Forest Lodge, and the Braes of Abernethy. From Forest Lodge the track goes south, through Ryvoan to Glenmore.

The Way ought not to be thought of as just another long-distance slog. In the first place it isn't all that long, and there is very little slogging, but it does offer many opportunities for many different kinds of walk. The Speyside Rambler bus makes it possible to walk individual sections and ride back to base, or to a waiting car.

For a selection of walks in this book see the following

chapters: Aberlour, Aviemore, Carrbridge, Cullen, Dufftown, Fochabers, Forres, Kincraig, Rothiemurchus and Tomintoul.
Some walking books are recommended in Further Reading.

PLEASE BE A SPEYSIDE FARMERS' FRIEND AND FOLLOW THE COUNTRY CODE:

Fasten all Gates
Keep to paths across farmland
Use gates and stiles to cross fences, hedges and walls
Take your litter home
Leave livestock, crops and machinery alone
Keep your dog under control
Guard against all risk of fire
Help to keep all water clean
Protect wildlife, plants and trees
Take care on country roads
Do not make un-necessary noise

Take Only Photographs And Leave Only Footprints

WATER SPORTS & OTHER ACTIVITIES

Water Rat observes in *The Wind in the Willows* that there is nothing - absolutely nothing - half so much worth doing as messing about in boats. A stroll along the shores of Loch Morlich or Loch Insh, or on the beach of Findhorn Bay, will rapidly confirm this assertion.

In an area seemingly designed to pander to lovers of the outdoor life, it should occasion no surprise to find that water sports enthusiasts have many opportunities for enjoyment. Water skiers are excluded from the lochs, but they can indulge themselves in Findhorn Bay. For the rest, there is plenty of scope for wind-surfing, sailing - both deep water and on the lochs, canoeing and, like Kenneth Graham's rat, simply messing about in boats.

It would be an odd world if everyone had the same interests, and as an 18th Cent. poet remarked: 'variety's the very spice of life'. Well, there is plenty of it here, and some very varied activities are on offer. For example, there are opportunities to sample the esoteric pleasures of 4x4 off-road driving in an All-Terrain Vehicle (A.T.V), clay pigeon shooting, deer stalking and rough shooting. Those who would like to trek, but don't get on with horses, can get their adrenalin flowing on an A.T.V. Finally, if all that is not enough, there is gliding in Spey Valley and the Laich of Moray.

CANOEING, SAILING, WINDSURFING & BOAT HIRE

Cairdsport, Loch Morlich, Aviemore - 0479 861221/810296

Locheil, Boat of Garten - 0479 83603

Loch Insh Watersports, Kincraig, Kingussie - 0540 661272

Moray Watersports, Findhorn - 0309 690239

Nairn Watersports, Lochloy Holiday Park, Nairn - 0667 55416

GLIDING

Cairngorm Gliding Club, Feshiebridge, Kingussie - 0540 651317

Highland Gliding Club, Birnie, Elgin - 0343 820834

OFF ROAD DRIVING & ALL TERRAIN VEHICLES (ATV)

Banchor Quads, Newtonmore - 0540 673711

Highland Drovers, Boat of Garten - 0479 83329

Landwise, Boat of Garten - 0479 83609

Rothiemurchus Estate, Inverdruie, Aviemore - 0479 810858

SHOOTING & STALKING

CLAY PIGEONS

Alvie Estate, Kincraig, Aviemore - 0540 651255

Landwise, Boat of Garten (laser) - 0479 83609

Rothiemurchus Estate, Inverdruie, Aviemore - 0479 810858

Stakis Coylumbridge Hotel, Aviemore (laser) - 0479 810661

Starshot, Glenrinnes Home Farm, Dufftown - 0340 20624

DEER STALKING

Alvie Estate, Kincraig - 0540 651255

GAME & ROUGH SHOOTING

Alvie Estate, Kincraig - 0540 651255

Craigellachie Hotel (residents), Craigellachie - 0340 881204

Delnashaugh Hotel (residents), Ballindalloch - 08072 255

WINTER SPORTS ON SPEYSIDE

An interesting social history could, no doubt, be written about the Victorians' urge to return to a countryside that had been so recently abandoned for the towns. The aristocracy had always enjoyed field sports, but this was different, and prosperous members of the middle classes - doctors, lawyers, parsons, and the like - who had the money and some spare time, took to the hills. The Scottish Mountaineering Club was formed in 1889.

A great deal of romantic excitment was engendered at the time by the exploits of people like Nansen, Bruce, Shackleton and Scott. The idea of trekking on skis across icy wastes caught the popular imagination, and some of the new hillmen realised that it could broaden the horizons of their winter week-ends. So, contrary to popular belief, skiing had become a popular Scottish pastime by the turn of the century. The Scottish Ski Club was formed by some winter-sporting members of the Mountaineering Club as long ago as 1907.

Those well-off Edwardians went by train to Spey Valley for skiing in the Monadhliaths. Between the wars, skiers travelled to Scotland by train and car in ever increasing numbers, and downhill skiing was developed in the deep, snow-holding mountain gullies. So popular was the sport that, by the mid-30's, there were fears about potential damage to the Ben Lawers area caused by excessive numbers. This era came to a juddering halt in 1939.

Speyside was busy during the war, and thousands of servicemen trained for mountain warfare in the local hills. When the war was over they had more leisure and more money than their pre-war counterparts, and they were determined to enjoy their new-found skills. The time was ripe for a boom in skiing, which was no longer the privilege of a few, and the first professional ski instructors appeared on the scene.

When Klaus Fuchs started his ski school at The Struan House Hotel in Carrbridge after the war, he revolutionised the local tourist industry. Other hotels in the area were quick to offer cheap skiing packages with instruction. Skiers wanted alpine-type equipment and facilities, and tows and lifts were installed at Lecht and Cairngorm. In a few years a completely new tourist industry developed, and it flourishes today.

Good spring snow was more consistent 30 - 40 years ago, and the sport was soon firmly established. Climate is a fickle thing, and snow cover seems much more variable now, but after a few bad seasons in recent years things are looking up again. The best snow seems to be in February and March, and there is often good cover at the beginning of December. Downhill and cross-country skiers are most affected by this. Off-piste skiers, out of the Edwardian mould, have a much better time of it, and high mountain snow cover can be around for half the year.

Many ski packages are on offer, and there are all sorts of facilities for equipment hire and instruction. The following is just a selection:

Badenoch Sports, Kingussie - 0540 661228: instuction & hire.

Cairdsport, Aviemore - 0479 810296: instruction & hire; dry slope.

Carrbridge Ski School - 0479 84246: instruction & hire.

Glenmore Shop, Glenmore - 0479 86253: hire; dry langlauf track.

Glenmulliach Nordic Ski Centre, Tomintoul - 08074 356: langlauf instruction & hire.

Insh Hall Ski Lodge, Kincraig - 0540 651: instruction & hire: dry slope.
Lecht Ski School, Lecht - 09756 51440: instruction & hire.
Nethybridge Ski School - 0479 82333: instruction & hire.
Nordic Ski Centre, Coylumbridge - 0479 810729: instruction & hire.
Norwest Ski School, Newtonmore - 0540 673771: instuction & hire; dry slope.
Scottish Youth Hostels Association - 031 229 8660: instruction.

SPEYSIDE CARAVAN & CAMPING SITES

Speyside is a superb area for a caravanning or camping holiday. It offers variety and easy travelling, and a reasonably large choice of sites. Locations vary from the mountains to the seaside, with a goodly mix of woodland and riverside in between. Some sites are virtually in the wilderness; others are near to towns. This selection is not claimed to be comprehensive but, whatever your requiremets, they can probably be satisfied from the many sites listed here. 'CC' denotes a caravan Club site. 'CCC' denotes a Caravan Club Certified site.

SPEY VALLEY

Aviemore, Campgrounds of Scotland, Coylumbridge - 0479 810120, S of A951/B970 junction at edge of Rothiemurchus forest 2 miles E of Aviemore. Vans & tents.

Aviemore, High Range CP - 0479 810636, W side of B9152 in village and S of Tourist Info. Centre. CCC.

Aviemore, Glenmore - 0479 86271, Forestry Commission site at Loch Morlich on road to Cairngorm chairlift. CCC. Vans & tents.

Boat of Garten, Campgrounds of Scotland - 0479 83652, at W edge of the village on R of road to Grantown/Aviemore. Vans & tents.

Boat of Garten, Croftnacarn - 0309 76628, on the Loch Garten road by B970 junction.

Grantown on Spey - 0479 2474, from Seafield Avenue

opposite bank of Scotland in town centre - follow signs. CCC. Vans & tents.

Kincraig, Dalraddy CP - 0479 810330, on Alvie estate 3 miles S of Aviemore on B9152. Between Aviemore and Kincraig. Vans & tents.

Kincraig, Insh House - 05404 377, S side of B970 by Loch Insh 2 miles S of Kincraig. CCC.

Kingussie, Columba House Hotel - 0540 661402, S side of High Street at E end of town. CCC.

Kingussie, Golf Club - 0540 661600, At golf club 1 mile N of town up Gynack Road.

Laggan Bridge, Blaragie - 05284 229, on minor road to Spey Dam 1 mile from Laggan Bridge. CCC.

Newtonmore, Invernahavon CP - 0540 673534, In Glen Truim on very minor road 3 miles S of Newtonmore. Vans & tents. CCC.

STRATHSPEY

Aberlour, Aberlour Gardens CP - 0340 871586, by the river near centre of village. Vans & tents.

Craigellachie, Elchies C & CP - 0340 6414, in an old prisoner-of- war camp off B9102 near Archiestown. Vans & tents.

Keith CP - 0343 545121, in Dunnyduff Road off A96 on S edge of town. Vans & tents.

SPEYMOUTH

Buckie, Strathlene - 0542 34851, on A942 between Buckie and Findochty. Vans & tents.

Burghead, Burghead CS - 0343 835618, by B9013 on S side of town & by West Beach. Vans & tents.

Cullen, Logie Park - 0343 545121, on the cliffs between the cemetery & playing fields at E end of town. Vans & tents.

Findochty CP - 0542 35303, W of harbour on sea front at end Jubilee Terrace. Vans & tents.

Fochabers, Burnside CP - 0343 820362, by A96 Keith Road S outskirts of town. Vans & tents.

Portknockie CP - 0542 40766, on MacLeod Park off Bridge Street at E end of town. Vans & tents.

Spey Bay CP - 0343 820424, by hotel & golf links at end of B9104. Vans & tents.

LAICH OF MORAY

Culloden - 0463 790625, on B9006 between Inverness & Croy. Vans and tents. CC.

Elgin, Riverside CP - 0343 542813, by the river on West Road (A96) - continuation of High Street. Vans & tents.

Elgin, North Alves CP - 034385 223, 1 mile N of Crook of Alves 6 miles W of Elgin on A96. Vans & tents.

Forres, Old Mill CP, Brodie - 03094 244, on S side of A96 at Brodie, 4 miles W of Forres. Vans & tents.

Findhorn, Findhorn Bay CP - 0309 690203, on B9011 road from Forres at entrance to village. Vans & tents.

Findhorn, Findhorn Sands CP - 0309 690324, in dunes between village and shore. Vans & tents.

Hopeman, Station CP - 0343 830880, near harbour and beach on W side of harbour road.

Lossiemouth, East Beach CP - 0343 545121, between the Lossie & Spynie Canal at Seatown S of town centre. Vans & tents.

Lossiemouth, Siver Sands CP - 0343 813262, near lighthouse at Covesea on B9040 2 miles W of Lossiemouth. Vans & tents.

Nairn, Blairnafade Farm - 06677 228, S of B9091 4 miles from Nairn. CCC.

Nairn, Alanaha Farm - 0667 53346, W of B9090 near B9091 junction 3 miles S of Nairn. CCC.

Nairn, Geddes House - 0667 52241, S of B9101 & between A939/B9090 3 miles S of Nairn. CCC.

Nairn, Lochloy CP, East Beach - **0667 52561**, at end of Harbour Street & by beach on E side of town. Vans & tents.

Nairn, Spindrift CP - **0667 53992**, At Little Kildrummie on minor road off B9090 3 miles S of Nairn. CCC.

INVERNESS

Ardersier, Hillhead Farm - **0667 62248**, On minor road off B9006 in Ardersier village. CCC.

Daviot, Auchnahillin C & CP - **046385 223**, by B9154 off A9 at Daviot, 8 miles S of Inverness.

Inverness, Torvean CP - **0463 220582**, by Glenurquhart Road (A82) & on banks of Caledonian Canal 1 mile SW of city centre.

FURTHER READING

The heyday of Speyside literature seems to have been the Victorian era, but most of what was written is now out of print. The following more recent books are worth searching for:

SPEYSIDE HISTORY

Culloden. John Prebble, Penguin Books. Arguably subjective, but undeniably a lucid and absorbing account of the greatest disaster to befall the Highlands.

Discovering Speyside. Francis Thompson, John Donald. ISBN 0 85976 230 0. An interesting introduction to Speyside, its people and their history.

History of Scotland. J D Mackie, Penguin. ISBN 0 1402 0671 X. A concise, readable and cheap popular history.

Memoirs of a Highland Lady - Volume 1. Elizabeth Grant, Canongate Press. ISBN 0 86241 396 6. Written in the 1860's for her children, edited by Lady Strachey and first published in 1898, these memoirs are a fascinating and wonderfully entertaining insight into Highland high society in the first 30 years of the 19th Cent. They make compulsive reading, and have long been a source book for historians. This abridged edition deals with her life in Strathspey.

NATURAL HISTORY

Wild Sports & Natural History of the Highlands, by Charles St. John was written in the mid 19th C. A timeless classic, much of the content is concerned with Speyside, and many of the observations are still relevant. A paperback edition was published in 1981 by Macdonald Futura. It is worth tracking down.

Seton Gordon wrote excellent books over a period of some 50 years from the 1920's on. Many of them are about the Cairngorms and their wildlife, and they can often be found in the second-hand market. They are all good reading.

The following more recent works may be of interest to readers who wish to delve more deeply into the subject. **The Cairngorms**. D Nethersole-Thompson and A Watson. New and enlarged edition, Melven Press, Perth. IBSN 0 906664 12 8. An exhaustive and very readable study of the physical features and natural history. A superb book, and it is very cheap.

Glenmore Forest Park - Cairngorms. Forestry Commission, HMSO 1975. This guide to the many attractions of the park is a "must" for anyone holidaying in the area. Fantastic value at £1.

Successful Nature Watching. Hall/Cleave/Sturry, Hamlyn 1985. ISBN 0 600 30602 X. One of a number of books on the subject, this is a useful guide to habitats and techniques, and is reasonably priced.

Collins' New Naturalist series has been re-issued by Bloomsbury Books. They are widely available at about £5. Incomparable books for those seriously interested in natural history. **Mountains and Moorlands**, by W H Pearsall, is especially recommended.

The Highlands and Islands Development Board have also published a series of large format paperbacks on specialist topics such as Birds, The Highlands, Mountain Flowers, etc. They cover the whole of the Highlands, and are well worth having.

WALKING & SKIING

Walks in the Cairngorms & **Short Walks in the Cairngorms**. Ernest Cross, Luath Press. ISBN 0 946487 09 X, 0 946487 23 5. Absolutely the best guides for walkers tackling these hills from Spey Valley. Concise, well produced and cheap.

Avonside Explored. Edward H. Peck, Edward H. Peck, Tomintoul 1989. ISBN 0 9508553 0 8. An enjoyable and informative guide to Strath Avon & Glenlivet. From the Visitor Centre, Tomintoul. **Scottish Skiing Handbook.** Hilary Park, Luath Press. ISBN 946487 20 0. The definitive guide to skiing in Scotland. Erudite, amusing and exhaustive, with hilarious cartoons by Bill Smith.

SPEYSIDE WILDLIFE

Speyside is absolutely bursting with wildlife, and it is as diverse and varied as the country, which ranges from the sub-arctic tundra of the Cairngorms, to the scrub and sand dunes of the coast. In between there is an interesting mixture of hills, lochs, river valleys, marshes, moors, ancient woodlands, pasture and arable land. This range of habitats is probably unique in Britain, and each one supports its own distinctive population. Many of the animals and birds are unusual, and some are peculiar to the region and occur nowhere else. The wild flowers may not be up to Ben Lawers standards, but they are varied and abundant.

These notes do not pretend to be anything other than a brief comment on the unusual. The natural history of the region has been the subject of several classic works, and they should be read by all those with more than just a passing interest in the area. Many books offer information about the area and its inhabitants, and some offer advice on observing them. As with many other things, an ounce of practice is worth a ton of theory, and the best thing is to go for a quiet walk and start looking.

It would be most unusual to spend any time in the hills in summer and not come across some red deer. Fences exclude them from much of the woodland, but they are occasionally seen in the old pine forests in winter. Opposite sexes live separate lives throughout most of the year and come together only in the breeding season, about October.

Roe deer live in small family groups, and are wholly creatures of the woodland. They are very common in Speyside woodlands, and they do a good deal of damage to seedling trees.

Reindeer are quite unlike other deer. Originally resident here in ancient times, they became extinct along with the wild boars and the wolves. Mr. Mikel Utse, a Swedish Lapp, reintroduced them some forty years ago. After a series of reverses the animals settled down on Cairngorm, and their numbers increased. The main herd now lives in the seclusion of Glenlivet because many Cairngorm animals died, having ingested rubbish left by visitors. Brief acquaintance will show why they are beloved by the Lapps. Normally they are delightfully friendly and gentle beasts, and they seem to like the company of people. Many of the local reindeer are busy at Christmas, and they go as far afield as the big London stores.

The pine marten, despite its name, is happy to live in any sort of woodland. Superficially like a polecat, it is larger, and has a white throat patch. A nocturnal hunter, it is unlikely to be seen, although it is not uncommon in the Speyside woods. The pine marten can become quite tame and one family, hooked on cake, regularly visits a Boat of Garten garden for a midnight feast.

A wild cat is not a domestic tabby gone wrong; it is a distinctive and very handsome breed of cat that is well established in Speyside. They are nocturnal and very shy, and unlikely to be seen other than by accident, or during a visit to the Wildlife Park at Kincraig.

Blue, or mountain, hares are smaller than their lowland cousins, and they assume a white coat for the winter. They seem to be quite rare now, but can be seen on the moors in Spey Valley and Glenlivet.

Grey squirrels have not yet arrived in the Highlands. The local red squirrels live in the pine woods, and their presence is shown by the pine cone 'cores' that litter the ground beneath the trees where they have fed. Squirrels leave a 'pineapple' top on the chewed cone, whist mice and other rodents eat it all.

Craig Dubh, behind Newtonmore, is famous for its wild goats, which look very like the ibex and wild goats of southern and eastern Europe. They are probably descended from domestic animals brought here by Bronze Age people, and will have reverted to the wild type over the ages. Like red deer, they live in separate herds until the autumn rut, when the billies become extremely agressive.

The haggis is a creature of the hills. A little furry animal with long legs, and a long nose and tail, it avoids people and is common only on the heathery slopes of the middle Monadhliaths and the uttermost Braes of Glenlivet. It is similar in many ways to the largely aquatic desmans of Russia and the Pyrenees, and it may have evolved from animals brought here as a food source by Bronze Age beaker people, in much the same way that the Romans introduced the dormouse.

The Scottish haggis *(haggis terrestis scoticus sinistrorsus)* is a sub-species of the type. It has the left legs slightly shorter than the right, which enables the animal to stand upright when progressing, as it normally does, anti-clockwise round the hill. The hunting season starts in December, and the usual method is to beat the hillside in a clockwise direction. The animals turn to escape, topple over, and roll to the bottom of the hill, where they are picked up by haggis baggers. A great delicacy, haggis is hung for a week, and is then skinned and boiled. Haggis is traditionally eaten on 25th January, accompanied by potatoes, turnips, whisky and bagpipe music.

The variety and number of birds are enormous. More than 250 different species have been recorded in Strathspey, and over 50 of these may be observed in the Abernethy RSPB reserve. Luck must play a part in the sighting of the rarities. The capercaille is a large and ungainly bird which does not seem to fly well. It is more likely to be heard than seen, and in flight it looks like a black or brown turkey (the hens are brown). The Speyside pine woods are all known habitats.

Blackcock were common many years ago, but now seem to be rare. They like to inhabit the country at forest margins, where old woodland gives way to pasture. Modern forestry, and the spread of new plantations, have reduced the area of this type of habitat, and this may be a reason for their decline. The Abernethy and Glenlivet woodlands would seem to be good places to look.

Crossbills, tree creepers, long tailed and crested tits, siskins and woodpeckers may all be observed in the woods, and it is impossible to ignore the chaffinches, which are everywhere. Some ornithologists maintain that the local birds have their own particular dialect.

Away from the woods, red grouse live on the lower hills, and ptarmigan occur above 3000 feet. Their nests are just scrapes in the ground, usually on the lee side of a rock. Golden eagles may be seen sometimes above Strath Nethy, the Lairig Ghru, the Feshie, and in the Monadhliaths, but people disturb them, and they have deserted the popular areas. Dotterel and snow bunting are to be seen on Cairngorm plateau above the head of Loch Avon.

At Craigellachie, behind the Aviemore Centre, there is one of the most consistently successful peregrine breeding sites in Britain, and it is comparatively easy to enjoy the thrilling and rewarding sight of one of these marvellous falcons in flight, perhaps returning with a kill. Many people travel long distances to see these birds, and it was a surprise to learn recently that Britain now has one of the major populations. It was said, for instance, that only seventy are left in the whole of France.

For many visitors the great attraction now is the ospreys, which sometimes seem to be everywhere. It may be a premature speculation, but their population seems to have increased quite rapidly and the number of birds arriving each spring is now into three figures. They are not all that uncommon now in Strathspey, and may be seen anywhere between Newtonmore and Tugnet.

The Insh Marshes are a famous habitat that supports a large and varied population of waders. Breeding wildfowl include wigeon, tufted duck and goldeneye, which are all present elsewhere along the

Spey. Sparrowhawks and hen harriers may be seen hunting over the riverside flats.

The coasts of Speymouth and the Laich of Moray are home to many seabirds. There are many sea ducks around the estuaries, and terns nest at various locations along the shore.

The plant life of the region is as varied as the terrain, and uncommon varieties at low level include lousewort, chickweed-wintergreen, twinflower, butterwort and sundews. Cow, crow and cloudberries, creeping azalea, alpine lady's mantle, saxifrages, moss campion, and a positively bewildering array of mosses and lichens may all be found at higher altitudes. There is a profusion of wild flowers at the waysides in summer.

The woodlands are a veritable paradise for entomologists, and they contain a wealth of moths, mosquitoes, midges, gnats, flies, mites, beetles, bugs, spiders, centipedes, millipedes, ants, and a whole host of weird and wonderful insects, many of them rare, and some of them to be found nowhere else. A famous naturalist was once asked if his life's work had taught him anything about God. "Yes", he is said to have replied, "He is inordinately fond of beetles"!

In the extensive woodlands of Strathspey one can see the point. the forest floor is, at first sight, virtually dead, and nothing much stirs on the surface other than ants, and ground, dung, tiger and rove beetles. But lift the litter a little and it is a totally different world: a savage and violent jungle, where eat or be eaten is the rule.

In the pinewoods the wood ants nests cannot be ignored, and these remarkable mounds of millions of pine needles house vast numbers of these busy creatures. Some of the nests are incredibly old; please do not disturb them, it could do irreparable harm.

Most people seem to actively dislike insects, and dismiss them all as 'creepy crawlies', which is sad, for they are all interesting. The exception, perhaps, is midges, which are very irritating in both senses of the word. Normally of interest only to anglers, fish, birds and bats, they can be an unmitigated and un-controllable nuisance to everybody else in July and August.

Speyside has many SSSI's and many nature reserves. These are administered by a bewildering variety of bodies, chief of which is **Scottish Natural Heritage**. Formed in 1992 by amalgamating The Countryside Commission for Scotland and the Nature Conservancy Council for Scotland, the new body should not be (but often is) confused with Historic Scotland, the sister body to English Heritage, who look after ancient monuments and some historic buildings.

Other important bodies are the **Royal Society for the Protection of Birds** and the **Scottish Wildlife Trust**, both of which have several important reserves in Speyside, and **Forest Enterprise**, the new and friendly face of the Forestry Commission, which is encouraging us to enjoy their extensive woodlands.

The Scottish Wildlife Trust has recently established a number of reserves in Speyside, which make an important contribution to the conservation of wildlife in the area. A charitable organisation, it is staffed largely by volunteers. Membership costs little, but the income it provides is vital to the continuation of the Trust's work. Further information can be had from:

Scottish Wildlife Trust,
25 Johnston Terrace,
EDINBURGH, EH1 2NH.

USEFUL INFORMATION

TOURIST INFORMATION

The Scots are rightly proud of Scotland, and it shows, and Scottish tourist information offices tend to be nothing less than superb. Well stocked, with all sorts of interesting publications and other items, they are staffed by local people who are, without exception, knowledgeable and keen to help. Local offices are shown on the map pages, and there are the following offices in England:

Southwaite Tourist Information Centre - 06974 73445: On the M6, about ten miles south of Carlisle. Operates the 'Book A Bed Ahead' service.

Scottish Tourist Board - 071 930 8661: The London office at 19 Cockspur Street, SW1Y 5BL. Near to Trafalgar Square.

LOCAL TOURIST ASSOCIATIONS

Aviemore & Spey Valley Tourist Board - 0479 810363

Grampian Road, Aviemore, PH22 1PP.

Inverness, Loch Ness & Nairn Tourist Board - 0463 234353

23 Curch Street, Inverness, IV1 1EZ.

Moray Tourist Board - 0343 542666

17 High Street, Elgin, IV30 1EG.

ACCOMMODATION

This does not normally present a problem, and there is adequate accommodation of all types and at all prices. The Tourist Associations produce excellent accommodation brochures, and the Book-a-bed-ahead scheme, operated by the main information centres, may be entirely adequate outside the peak summer months and the popular Bank Holiday weekends.

The Scottish Youth Hostels Association has five hostels in the area, mainly in Spey Valley. They are very popular with foreign visitors, and are not just for the young in years. The hostel at Loch Morlich is unusual in that it serves meals, which are of legendary quality. It is also the base for some excellent skiing and watersports instruction package holidays. Hostels at Aviemore, Inverness, Kingussie, Loch Morlich & Tomintoul. Details: SYHA, 7 Glebe Crescent, Stirling, FK8 2JA.

EATING & DRINKING

The area is famous for its salmon, trout, venison and other game, and Aberdeen Angus beef, which actually comes from Speyside, is world renowned. Eating and drinking is often a delight, and in the smaller towns and villages the hotels and restaurants often specialise in traditional cuisine. Scottish cooking is famous, and some of the dishes evidently owe something to The Auld Alliance with France. Do sample the Scottish 'high tea'. Once common all over Britain, it is now virtually confined to Scotland. Normally served between afternoon tea and dinner times, it is usually a satisfying and substantial repast.

ACCESS

There are few official rights of way, but the Scots have a very liberal attitude to people walking across their land, although some of the incomers from outwith Scotland can have an odd attitude. A common misconception is that there is no law of trespass in Scotland. In fact there is, but it is not something that people get het up about. If in doubt, ask, and permission will usually be granted. There are restricted areas on the hills during the deer cull - roughly from mid-August to the end of October. Details from information centres - This is important!